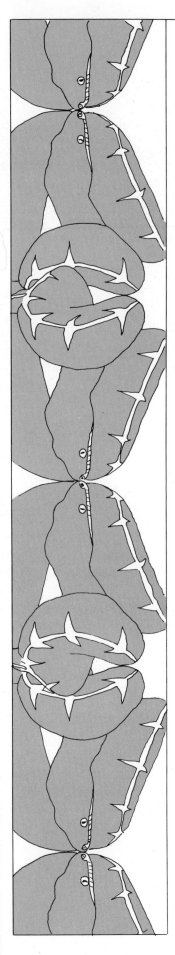

A Close-Up Look At Let's Hear It For Herps!

L ooking at the Table of Contents, you can see we've divided *Let's Hear It for Herps!* into four chapters (each of which deals with a broad herp theme), a craft section, and an appendix. Each of the four chapters includes *background information* that explains concepts and vocabulary, *activities* that relate to the chapter theme, and *Copycat Pages* that reinforce many of the concepts introduced in the activities.

You can choose single activity ideas or teach each chapter as a unit. Either way, each activity stands by itself and includes teaching objectives, a list of materials needed, suggested age groups, subjects covered, and a step-by-step explanation of how to do the activity. (The objectives, materials, age groups, and subjects are highlighted in the left-hand margin for easy reference.)

Age Groups
The suggested age groups are:
- Primary (grades K-2)
- Intermediate (grades 3-5)
- Advanced (grades 6-7)

Each chapter begins with primary activities and ends with intermediate and advanced activities. But don't feel bound by the grade levels we suggest. You'll be able to adapt many of the activities to fit your particular age group and needs.

Outdoor Activities
We've included several outdoor activities in this issue. These are coded in the chapters in which they appear with this symbol:

Copycat Pages
The *Copycat Pages* supplement the activities and include ready-to-copy games, puzzles, coloring pages, and/or worksheets. Look at the bottom of each Copycat Page for the name and page number of the activity that it goes with. *Answers to all Copycat Pages are in the texts of the activities.*

What's At The End
The fifth section, *Crafty Corner*, will give you some art and craft ideas that complement many of the activities in the first four chapters. And the last section, the *Appendix*, is loaded with reference suggestions that include books, films, and posters. The *Appendix* also has a glossary and suggestions for where to get more reptile and amphibian information.

MEET THE HERPS

Some can go without a meal for more than a year. Others can live for a century—and not really reach a ripe old age for another couple of decades or so. There's one species with a gestation period of up to 38 months, and another whose 2-inch (5-cm) body contains enough poison to kill hundreds of people. What kinds of animals are these? They're *herps*—the collective name given to reptiles and amphibians.

SORTING IT ALL OUT

The word "herp" comes from the word "herpetology," the branch of zoology that focuses on reptiles and amphibians. (*Herpeton* is the Greek word for "crawling things.") Four major groups—lizards, worm-lizards, and snakes; turtles; crocodilians; and the tuatara—make up the reptiles. And amphibians are represented by three groups: frogs; salamanders; and the obscure, wormlike creatures known as caecilians (see-SIL-ee-ans).

A Classy Bunch: Even though reptiles and amphibians are grouped together for study, they're two very different kinds of animals. They're related in the sense that early reptiles evolved from amphibians—just as birds, and later, mammals, evolved from reptiles. (See "Herps, Past and Present" on page 6 for more about ancient herps.) But reptiles and amphibians are each in a class by themselves—just as, for example, mammals are in their own separate class. (A *class* is a broad, scientific grouping of organisms with similar features.)

One of the reasons reptiles and amphibians are lumped together under the heading of "herps" is that, at one time, naturalists thought the two kinds of animals were much more closely related than they really are—and the practice of studying them together just persisted through the years.

Reptiles vs Amphibians: Many of the differences between reptiles and amphibians are internal. For example, a reptile's circulatory system and some of its skeletal features are quite different from those of an amphibian. And most reptiles have a better developed lung capacity, resulting in a more efficient respiratory system. But these two groups do have some noticeable external differences too. Most reptiles have claws on their feet and dry skin covered with scales. And most amphibians have clawless feet and moist, scaleless skin. Another difference has to do with eggs and development. Most amphibians lay soft, shell-less eggs in water, and the young usually reach adulthood after passing through a change called *metamorphosis.* Reptiles, on the other hand, usually lay shelled eggs on land. And when their eggs hatch, the young look like miniature adults. As a rule, reptiles also lay fewer eggs than amphibians do. (For more about the characteristics of each of these groups, see pages 19-22 and 36-39.)

WHAT MAKES A HERP A HERP?

Even though reptiles and amphibians are different from each other in many ways, they do have certain important characteristics in common. Here's a look at a few of these characteristics:

External Energy: All reptiles and amphibians are *ectothermic,* or cold-blooded. This means that unlike *endothermic,* or warm-blooded animals (i.e., birds and mammals), herps can't generate enough body heat to maintain a constant temperature. Instead, reptiles and amphibians must depend on an external energy

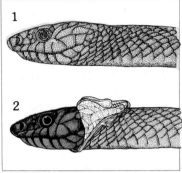

snake starting to shed its skin

source to provide their bodies with the heat energy they need to function efficiently. To warm up so they can be active, many herps bask in the sun or sit in warm water. And not surprisingly, most herps are sluggish or inactive on cold days. Endothermic animals, on the other hand, generate enough body heat to stay relatively active even when the temperature around them is low. They don't need to rely on external sources to keep their body temperatures up to a "workable" level.

Being ectothermic does have its advantages, though. For example, herps don't need to provide their bodies with the quantity of "fuel" required to maintain a constant temperature. So they don't need to eat as much as birds and mammals do and they can go without food for longer periods of time. And many can live in places that don't have enough food resources to support birds and mammals. (*Note:* Many people prefer to use endothermic and ectothermic, rather than warm-blooded and cold-blooded, to describe how animals regulate and maintain their body temperatures. That's because the terms "cold-blooded" and "warm-blooded" can be misleading if they're not explained. For example, cold-blooded animals don't actually have cold blood.)

Growing Out of Their Skin: If you spend much time hiking in natural areas, you've probably come across the dry, thin, outermost layer of skin that a snake left behind when it shed. Most other herps also shed their skin from time to time—usually several times a year, depending on how quickly the animal grows. You'd have a tough time finding other herps' skin, though. That's because many herps eat their shed skins, which are a good source of protein.

Herps of a Different Color: Another feature of herps' skin is its ability to change color. Pigment-containing skin cells called *chromatophores* are responsible for color change, and they're usually triggered into action by the temperature, humidity, and/or amount of light in a herp's surroundings. For example, cool temperatures usually cause chromatophore pigments to spread out, and the reptile or amphibian becomes a darker shade of its existing color. Warm temperatures usually have the opposite effect: They cause chromatophore pigments to contract, which causes a herp's color to become lighter. (A few herps can become a different color altogether. For example, some chameleons can change from green to brown, and vice versa.)

A herp's "emotional state"—i.e., fear, nervousness, and so on—can also cause chromatophores to expand or contract. And in some cases so can the color of a herp's surroundings. Chameleons, for example, can become almost invisible by matching the color of the vegetation around them. This ability isn't a conscious effort on the part of the lizard. It's just an automatic response to conditions in the animal's environment.

How Herps Smell: Have you ever wondered why certain snakes and lizards flick their tongues in and out? They're smelling the environment. As a herp's tongue flicks out, it collects molecules from the air and ground and deposits some of them in the paired sensory pockets of the *Jacobson's organ* at the back of the mouth. The Jacobson's organ analyzes the molecules and sends messages to the herp's brain.

Most herps have a Jacobson's organ, though it's not always well developed. And not all of the herps with a Jacobson's organ collect the molecules on their tongues. Some salamanders, for example, collect them through their nostrils. But regardless of how the information is gathered, a Jacobson's organ is helpful to herps in a lot of ways. Among other things, it's useful in tracking down prey, finding a mate, and avoiding predators and toxic substances.

A HISTORY OF HERPS

Scientists have traced the history of herps back about 360 million years—to the swampy forests of the Devonian Period. It was during this time that amphibians became the first vertebrates to colonize the land—a major step in the evolution of vertebrate life.

Lobe-fins Lead the Way: The direct ancestors of the amphibians were probably a group of fish known as the lobe-fins. Lobe-fins had several characteristics that other fish didn't have—including lungs (in addition to gills) and fins on their abdomen that were supported by bone. (Other fish had fins supported by "weaker" cartilage.) Scientists think these characteristics facilitated the gradual move of vertebrates onto land. The fish could use their lungs to breathe air and use their fins to support their weight in shallow water. Some scientists think that lobe-fins might have even been able to pull themselves across the land in search of deeper water.

Land of Opportunity: Evolution favored the amphibians' development for several reasons. At the time, there wasn't much competition on land, since certain insects and other invertebrates were the only animals that had managed to colonize it. And unlike the teeming waters, land habitats were virtually free from predators. Plus, the land-dwelling insects, spiders, and other invertebrates were an untapped source of food.

With such a rich world available to them, the new amphibians "took over." They spread out into the swampy forests, adapting to the conditions of the time. Some of these early amphibians were huge by today's standards—as large as or larger than a good-sized crocodile. (By contrast, most modern amphibians are less than six inches [15 cm] long.)

The Water Connection: For 100 million years or more, amphibians were the dominant animals on land. But even though they didn't have much competition, they did depend on specific habitat conditions in order to survive. They required a wet (or at least moist) environment for laying their eggs. And most needed to stay moist themselves in order to "breathe," or respire, through their skin, and to prevent dehydration.

Over time, some forms of amphibians evolved that were somewhat less dependent on water than their predecessors. And although scientists haven't been able to find all of the fossil pieces to the puzzle, they believe that these particular amphibians were the ancestors of the reptiles. The reptiles evolved over a period of many millions of years—and by at least 260 million years ago, they had definitely "arrived."

The Reptiles' Reign: This new group of animals was far less dependent on water than amphibians. For example, their shelled eggs were naturally protected from drying out—so they didn't have to be laid in water. And reptile skin didn't need to stay moist, since respiration wasn't one of its functions and scales kept the animals from becoming dehydrated.

Armed with these and other advantages, reptiles populated habitats that previously had been unavailable to land vertebrates. One group of reptiles, the dinosaurs, eventually became the "rulers" of the Earth. And they held on to that title for more than 160 million years, until some mysterious series of events caused their downfall.

python skeleton
artesy of the American Museum of Natural History

Herps, Past and Present

Take a look at some ancient reptiles and amphibians.

___

Objective:
Describe an ancient reptile or amphibian.

Ages:
Primary

Materials:
- *copies of page 15*
- *pictures of amphibians and reptiles*
- *string (optional)*

Subjects:
Science and Language Arts

If you could travel back in time about 80 million years, you'd see some pretty surprising reptiles. For example, you might run into *Deinosuchus*, a dinosaur-eating crocodile that was more than 50 feet (15 m) long. Or you might spot *Archelon*, a sea turtle with a 12-foot (3.5-m) long shell. In this activity your kids can learn about these and other amazing ancient reptiles, along with the amphibians that preceded them. (For more information on the evolution of reptiles and amphibians, see "A History of Herps" on page 5.)

Begin by showing the kids pictures of some familiar amphibians and reptiles. Then tell the kids that millions of years ago, many different kinds of amphibians and reptiles lived on the Earth. But many of these ancient herps looked a lot different from the ones that we see today.

Next pass out copies of page 15. Explain that these pictures show some ancient reptiles and amphibians in the places where they lived. Also point out that none of these animals is alive today.

Then ask the kids questions about each amphibian or reptile to get them thinking about these ancient animals. For example, you could ask them what they noticed first about the animal, how they think it got around, what it might have eaten, and if the animal reminds them of any modern herps. You might also ask them to think of some words to describe the animal. Then use the information below to discuss each amphibian or reptile. The kids can also practice saying each name out loud.

Afterward you may want to take the kids outside and compare some familiar objects with the dimensions of these ancient herps. For example, you could compare a pteranodon's wingspan to the length of a school bus. Or you could have the kids do some simple measurements, such as stretching out a 50-foot (15-m) piece of string to give them an idea of the size of *Deinosuchus*.

HERPS FROM LONG AGO

Diplocaulus

Pteranodon (tair-AN-uh-don) was a flying reptile that lived about 80 million years ago. Its wings spanned 26 feet (8 m)—almost as long as a school bus. *Pteranodon* probably lived near the sea and dove into the water to catch fish.

Elasmosaurus (ee-LAZ-muh-SAWR-us) lived in the sea about 80 million years ago. It belonged to a group of early reptiles called plesiosaurs. Its body was about 39 feet (12 m) long, and its neck made up half that length. *Elasmosaurus* had four long, flat flippers that it used to paddle through the water. With its long neck, it could quickly dart out its head and catch fish with its needle-sharp teeth.

Ichthyostega (ICK-thee-oh-STAY-ga), one of the earliest amphibians, first appeared about 345 million years ago. Although it could walk on land using its four strong legs, it probably spent a lot of time in the water. Its strong, flat tail moved back and forth to propel it through the water. *Ichthyostega* was about 3 feet (1 m) long and ate insects and other small animals.

Diplocaulus (dip-lo-CALL-us) was a water-dwelling amphibian that lived about 270 million years ago. Its long tail helped move its 3-foot (1-m) long body through the water. Scientists aren't sure how this early amphibian used its strange horned head. They think it could have been used for defense against predators. *Diplocaulus*

lived in lagoons and other swampy areas and ate fish, insects, and small amphibians.

Mastodonsaurus (MAS-tuh-don-SAWR-us) lived about 200 million years ago. This amphibian was about 13 feet (4 m) long. It probably spent most of its time in swamps and ate insects and other small animals.

Archelon (AR-kee-lon), the biggest sea turtle in history, lived about 90 million years ago. Its shell was about 12 feet (3.5 m) long. That's about twice as long as a leatherback sea turtle—the largest sea turtle in the world today. *Archelon* ate fish and other aquatic animals.

Tyrannosaurus (tye-RAN-o-SAWR-us) lived about 70 million years ago and was about 39 feet (12 m) long. Scientists think that this 6-ton (5-t), meat-eating dinosaur chased its prey on its strong hind legs. Its six-inch (15-cm) teeth helped it tear apart its prey.

Deinosuchus (dye-no-SOOK-us), an early crocodile, grew to be about 52 feet (16 m) long. (The record for a modern crocodile is 28 feet [8 m].) *Deinosuchus* lived about 75 million years ago and probably ate small dinosaurs.

Hands-On Herps

Learn about the general characteristics of reptiles and amphibians by visiting several "herp stations."

Objectives:
Describe some general characteristics of reptiles and amphibians. Talk about the ways the two groups are alike and different.

Ages:
Primary, Intermediate, and Advanced

Materials:
- *chalkboard or easel paper*
- *index cards*
- *paper*
- *pencils*
- *pictures of reptiles and amphibians (optional)*
- *tables*
- *for other materials, see the suggestions listed with each demonstration*

Subject:
Science

H ere's a hands-on way to help your kids learn about the general characteristics of reptiles and amphibians. Before you begin the activity, set up the "herp stations" described below and on page 8. Also copy each of the instructions shown in color on a separate index card and place the cards at the appropriate stations. (It's best to set up the stations along a few tables to give the kids enough room to work. After setting up, cover or move the tables so that the kids can't see what's on them.)

Note: You can adapt this activity according to the age of your group. For example, if you're working with younger kids, you may want to eliminate stations 5 and 6. We've also included some simpler options at the other stations for younger groups. And if you're working with very young kids, you could "explore" stations 1-4 as a group.

Start the activity by writing the words "reptile" and "amphibian" on a chalkboard or piece of easel paper. Ask the kids to name as many different kinds of reptiles and amphibians as they can think of, and list their suggestions under the proper heading. You can also show them pictures of different herps to give them ideas.

Now tell the kids they'll be learning about the general characteristics of reptiles and amphibians by visiting several stations. Divide the group into pairs and give each pair a piece of paper and a pencil.

Have each pair start at a different station. Give them time to follow the instructions on the index card and write their answer on their paper. Then, on your signal, have them change stations. Continue switching until everyone has visited all the stations.

Afterward gather the group together and go over the answers using the discussion information under "Sorting Out the Stations" on page 9. Based on what the kids learned at the stations, make a list of reptile characteristics and another list of amphibian characteristics. What do the groups have in common? What makes them different? (See pages 3-4 for more about the characteristics of reptiles and amphibians.)

Luise Woelflein

Station #1
SCALES vs SLIME
Materials: A piece of clay with rows of shelled sunflower seeds stuck in it (labeled A). (See page 42 for an illustration of seeds and clay.) A piece of cellophane covered with a thin layer of vegetable oil (labeled B).

Run your finger over material A and then material B. Make a short list of words that describe how each one feels. Which one do you think represents reptile skin and which one represents amphibian skin?

For younger kids: Tell them that material A represents reptile skin and B represents amphibian skin. Then have them feel and describe both materials.

(continued next page)

Station #2
EGGS
Materials: Tapioca sprinkled in a container filled with water (labeled A). A few grapes laid on sand or dirt (labeled B).

Feel the material floating in A and the objects in B. Describe some differences between them. Which ones do you think represent amphibian eggs and which ones represent reptile eggs?
For younger kids: Tell them which objects represent reptile eggs and which represent amphibian eggs, then let them feel each kind. Discuss the differences between the two kinds of eggs.

Station #3
CHANGING COLORS
Materials: A black pipe cleaner taped to a piece of black construction paper (labeled A). A yellow pipe cleaner taped to a piece of black construction paper (labeled B). Tape A and B to a wall about 10 feet (3 m) away from the station.

Which is harder to see, the black pipe cleaner or the yellow pipe cleaner? The colors of some reptiles and amphibians can change. For example, some lizards can change from green to brown. How might this help the lizards survive?
For younger kids: Have them point out the one that is harder to see and discuss their answers.

Station #4
BACKBONES
Materials: Copy of page 49 (optional).

Reach around and feel the middle of your back. What bones do you feel? Which of the groups listed below have similar bones in their back? (You can choose more than one answer.)
  a. snakes
  b. insects
  c. salamanders
  d. frogs
For younger kids: Show the kids page 49 and have them guess what it is. (a snake skeleton) Let them feel their backbones, then discuss the fact that all vertebrates, including all reptiles and amphibians, have backbones and internal skeletons.

Station #5
COLD-BLOODED CREATURES
Materials: Copy the two graphs below and label them as shown. Also write down the definitions of *cold-blooded* and *warm-blooded* (see the glossary on page 67).

Graph A shows the body temperature of an animal during one day, and Graph B shows the body temperature of another animal during the same day. What is different about the body temperatures of the two animals? Now read the definitions of cold-blooded and warm-blooded. Can you tell which graph shows the body temperature of a lizard? How did you know?

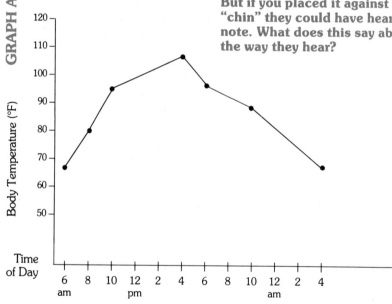

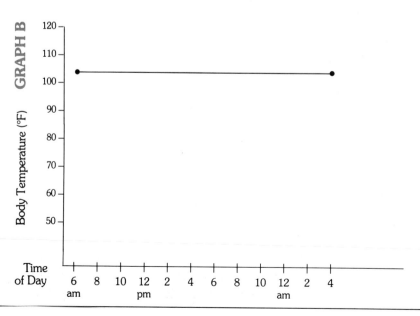

Station #6
HEAR THOSE VIBRATIONS
Materials: A tuning fork. *Note:* You may want to demonstrate how to listen to the tuning fork before the kids try it. And to avoid scratching the tuning fork, make sure the kids don't tap it on a metal surface.

Hold the tuning fork by the stem and tap it on a wooden chair or table. (Be careful not to touch the two prongs after hitting the fork on the table.) Then hold it next to your ear. Now tap it again and this time place the base of the stem against your chin. (Press it hard!) Describe what happens each time.

Some reptiles and amphibians would not have been able to hear anything if you held the tuning fork near the side of their head. But if you placed it against their "chin" they could have heard the note. What does this say about the way they hear?

8

1. The cellophane covered with oil represents the moist, glandular skin of most amphibians. The clay with seeds in it represents the dry, scaly skin of most reptiles. Point out that not all herps fit these generalizations—for example, many toads have fairly dry, rough skin. And some geckos have smooth skin with inconspicuous scales.

2. The tapioca represents the jellylike feel of amphibian eggs. Explain that amphibian eggs don't have shells, so they don't have much natural protection against drying out. But most amphibian eggs stay moist because they're laid in water or moist areas on land. Then explain that the grapes represent shelled reptile eggs. (Most reptile eggs are firm, like grapes, but not brittle like bird eggs.) Because they have shells, reptile eggs can survive in drier areas than amphibian eggs can.

   Point out that different types of reptiles lay different kinds of eggs. For example, turtle eggs are usually round and have a smooth shell. But many snake eggs are oval and often feel leathery. Also tell the kids that although most herps lay eggs, some do bear live young.

3. The black pipe cleaner (A) should be harder to see. Being able to blend in with their surroundings can help amphibians and reptiles get within striking distance of their prey. And it can help them hide from predators.

   Being able to change color also helps some amphibians and reptiles control their body temperatures. For example, when in direct sunlight, the skin of many herps becomes lighter. Since light-colored surfaces don't absorb as much heat as dark-colored surfaces do, this ability to change color can keep herps from overheating.

4. The kids should feel the vertebrae that form their backbones. All reptiles and amphibians, including snakes, salamanders, and frogs, are vertebrates. Like birds and mammals, herps have backbones and internal skeletons. But invertebrates, such as insects, do not have an internal skeleton. Instead, they have a hard outer covering called an *exoskeleton*.

5. The body temperature of the animal in Graph A changed over time. The body temperature of the animal in Graph B remained the same throughout the day. Graph A represents the body temperature of a cold-blooded animal, such as a lizard, and Graph B represents the body temperature of a warm-blooded animal, such as a bird. Point out that birds and mammals are warm-blooded animals, whereas reptiles, amphibians, and fish are cold-blooded. (For more about warm- and cold-blooded animals, see "External Energy" on page 3.)

6. The kids should have heard the same sound each time. The reason they heard a sound when they held the fork to their chin is that vibrations traveled through the bones in their jaw and skull to the fluid in their inner ear. Here the vibrations were "translated" into nerve impulses and interpreted as "sound" by the brain.

   Most herps, as well as most vertebrates, can detect sound in this way. (In many herps, the jawbone is most sensitive to ground vibrations.) Birds, mammals, and most reptiles and amphibians also have external ears that pick up sound waves in the air. But some herps, such as snakes and salamanders, don't have outer ears, and rely on vibrations to "hear" what's going on.

Herps on Stage

Take part in a play that emphasizes the characteristics of amphibians and reptiles.

Objective:
Give an example of a characteristic that reptiles and amphibians have in common and a characteristic that makes them different.

Ages:
Intermediate

Materials:
- *copies of pages 16 and 17*

(continued next page)

Putting on a puppet play can be a fun way for your kids to review the characteristics of amphibians and reptiles. Begin by using the background information on pages 3–5 to go over the major characteristics and evolutionary history of amphibians and reptiles. Point out that although these animals are often lumped together as "herps," they are actually two separate groups.

Next tell the kids that they'll be taking part in a puppet play about herps. Assign them the parts listed under "Cast of Characters" on page 16 and explain that they'll be making puppets to portray their characters. Show the kids pictures of these amphibians and reptiles for reference, then have them follow the directions on page 10 to make their puppets. Next pass out copies of pages 16 and 17 so the kids can read over their lines.

Also see the section titled "Tips for Putting on the Play," below. Afterward review the characteristics of reptiles and amphibians with the kids.

TIPS FOR PUTTING ON THE PLAY

- Have the kids use their scripts during the play so they don't have to memorize their lines.
- To make a stage, put two long tables end to end and drape sheets or some other kind of

- pictures of reptiles and amphibians
- rulers or wooden dowels
- thin cardboard
- light-colored knee socks
- construction paper
- tape and glue
- crayons or markers
- stapler and scissors
- tables and sheets

Subjects:
Science and Drama

material over them. The kids can crouch or sit behind the tables. Have the kids with sock puppets rest their arms on the tables. The other puppeteers can sit a bit farther away from the stage and hold up their arms so the audience can see the puppets.
- All the puppets should be on stage throughout the play. You may want to posi-

tion the chairperson away from the rest of the crowd and have the narrator sit to one side of the stage.
- As they say their lines, have the players move their puppets around so the audience can tell who's "talking."
- Encourage the kids to add sound effects such as "ribbits" and "croaks."

MAKING SOCK AND STICK PUPPETS

Sock Snakes and Caecilians
Puppets made from knee socks work best for the snake and caecilian characters. Here's how to make them:
1. Make a "mouth" by putting your hand in the foot of a light-colored sock (see drawing).
2. Figure out where the eyes should be placed on the snake and caecilian. Mark these points with a crayon or marker before taking off the sock. Also figure out where the snake's tongue should go.

3. Cut out eyes and a tongue from construction paper and glue them in place. Color the body with crayons or markers to resemble the real animal.

Cardboard Characters
The rest of the characters are easier to make with cardboard and wooden supports.
1. Fold a piece of thin cardboard in half and sketch the character on one side.
2. Holding the cardboard halves together, cut along the lines of the drawing so that you have two copies of the puppet.
3. Staple the two halves together along the edges of the cardboard, but leave the base of the puppet open.
4. Color both sides of the puppet.
5. Place the end of a ruler or wooden dowel into the base of the puppet and use tape to keep it from slipping.
6. You can also cover the ruler or dowel with black construction paper to disguise it.

Hot 'n' Cool Herps

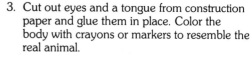

Keep a "thermometer lizard" within a certain temperature range.

Objectives:
Define the terms cold-blooded, warm-blooded, ectotherm, and endotherm. Describe the behaviors that some reptiles and amphibians use to regulate their body temperatures.

Ages:
Intermediate and Advanced

Materials:
- *sunny day*
- *thermometers with metal backings*
- *slips of paper*
- *chalkboard or easel paper*

Some reptiles and amphibians keep their body temperatures within a "preferred" temperature range. For example, the desert iguana usually keeps its temperature between 104° and 106° F (40° and 41° C), and the rose-bellied lizard's temperature usually doesn't vary more than a degree or two from 98° F (37° C). How do they do it?

Most herps use a variety of techniques, such as basking in the sun when cool and retreating to shade or burrowing underground when hot, to stay within their preferred range. In this activity your kids can use "thermometer lizards" to discover for themselves how herps control their body temperatures. (*Note:* This activity will work best on a sunny day.) Here's how to do it:

GETTING READY

1. Choose an area with a mixture of sunny and shady places. There should be enough room for the kids to spread out. Take temperatures around the area to find the lowest and highest temperatures. Allow enough time for the thermometer readings to stabilize (about two minutes) before you record the temperatures. (*Note:* The highest and lowest temperatures should be

taken no more than one hour from the time that the kids start using their thermometers.)
2. Next decide on a series of five-degree temperature ranges. The lower limit of the first range should be five degrees below the coldest temperature you recorded. (For example, if your lowest temperature was 60° F, the first range would be 55-59° F.) Continue making

ndian house gecko

non-overlapping five-degree ranges until you've reached a temperature that is five degrees warmer than the highest temperature you recorded (see example in lower margin).
3. Assign each temperature range to an imaginary lizard (for example, Lizard A would have a temperature interval of 55-59° F). Then copy each lizard's let-

ter and its temperature range on a separate slip of paper.
4. Later you'll assign a range to each pair of kids in your group. If you have a large group, you can assign more than one pair to a range. And if you have more ranges than pairs of kids, leave out some of the middle ranges.

INTRODUCING YOUR KIDS TO THE LIZARDS

Use the information under "External Energy" on page 3 and the information under "The Ups and Downs of Temperature Control" on page 12 to discuss the terms *cold-blooded, warm-blooded, ectotherm,* and *endotherm* and how they relate to amphibians and reptiles. Then divide the kids into pairs and tell them that each pair will pretend their thermometer is a different type of lizard. Also explain what a preferred temperature range is and what happens if a lizard gets too hot or cold. Be sure to point out that although many herps have a preferred range, the kids will be focusing on lizards because they're some of the "best" temperature regulators. But also explain that not all lizards have a narrow preferred range.

Next give each team a thermometer and one of the lizard slips that you made earlier. Tell the kids that they will be going

outside to try to find places where they can keep their lizards within their preferred range.

Ask the kids if they can think of some ways to regulate their lizard's body temperature. (Encourage them to be creative, but don't tell them what techniques to use.) The kids may come up with ideas such as putting the thermometer in direct sun; alternating it between shade and sun; keeping it in cool, shady areas; putting it underground; or looking for areas with no grass that will be very hot.

Also point out that, depending on their lizard's range, they'll probably have to use different techniques to stay within range. Some teams might be able to find one spot and stay there, but others may have to move from place to place to keep their temperatures in range. And some may not be able to stay within their range at all.

**lowest temperature
measured: 60° F
highest temperature
measured: 100° F**

RANGES (° F)
  55-59
  60-64
  65-69
  70-74
  75-79
  80-84
  85-89
  90-94
  95-99
  100-104
  105-109

LIZARDS IN ACTION

Have the teams spread out over the area and start taking temperatures. Emphasize that they should get their temperatures within their preferred range and keep them in range until time is up. (You may want to set a time limit of about 10 minutes for the teams to get within range.)

Give them these tips to follow as they take temperatures:

• Leave the thermometers in place for at least a minute so they will register an accurate temperature.
• Touch only the metal backing, not the bulbs of the thermometers.
• Keep the thermometers close to the ground or other surfaces to avoid taking air temperatures.

BACK INSIDE: WHO MADE IT?

Copy the chart in the upper margin of the next page on a chalkboard or piece of easel paper. Then fill in the information as a group, using the following questions to discuss what happened.

• Which lizards were able to stay within their preferred range? Have the "successful" pairs describe how they kept their thermometers within range.

(continued next page)

- Which lizards might have a tough time surviving in your area? (The ones with the lowest ranges probably couldn't survive above ground, and the ones with the highest ranges might find even the open areas to be too cool.)
- Depending on the time of year and where you live, some lizards may have been assigned temperature ranges as high as 120–124° F (49–51° C). Ask the kids if they think many real lizards have a preferred temperature range that's so high. (No. Most lizards can't survive if their body temperature reaches more than 115° F [46° C]. And if they can, it's only for a short time.)
- If none of the teams tried less obvious techniques, such as placing their thermometer lizards underground or under leaves, take them back outside for another try after the discussion. For example, have them take temperatures at different ground depths, and see if the team with the lowest temperature interval could stay "in-bounds" by burrowing.

SAMPLE CHART

LIZARD	RANGE (°F)	DID IT STAY IN RANGE?	WHERE DID YOU PUT IT?
A	55-59	no	under a bush
B	60-64	yes	in shady grass

THE UPS AND DOWNS OF TEMPERATURE CONTROL

- Most amphibians and reptiles instinctively keep their body temperatures within a specific temperature range. This is called their *preferred range* or *normal activity range*. To be active (i.e., find and digest food, escape from predators, and so on) a herp must stay within this range. If its body gets too hot or too cold, the animal won't function as well as it should. And if its body temperature goes above a *critical maximum* or below a *critical minimum,* it won't be able to move at all and will eventually die from the extreme temperature.
- A herp's preferred temperature range is related to where it lives. Reptiles and amphibians that live in cooler places, such as high altitude forests, have lower preferred ranges. And those with higher preferred ranges are found in warmer areas, such as deserts.
- In general, amphibians have lower preferred ranges than reptiles. And many amphibians don't keep their body temperatures as constant as some reptiles do.
- Many reptiles, especially some lizards, have narrow preferred ranges and behave in ways that keep their bodies at an almost constant temperature.

Luise Woelflein

TEMPERATURE TACTICS

Different kinds of herps use different combinations of the "tactics" listed below to stay within their preferred range. For example, most snakes can't change color, but they do burrow and/or bask.

Sun and Shade: Alternating between hot, sunny areas and cool, shady spots is the most common way that reptiles control their body temperature.

Many amphibians also bask in the sun to warm up. But, since they are vulnerable to water loss through their skin, amphibians usually bask only if they're in a moist place where they can replenish lost water.

It's All in the Timing: Some herps are active only when the temperature is "right." For example, many desert-dwelling reptiles are active at night or in the early morning to avoid scorching daytime temperatures.

Underground: Many amphibians and reptiles retreat to cool burrows when daytime temperatures get too hot. They also go underground at night, when burrows are warmer than the air above ground.

Color Changes: By changing the color of their skin, many herps can adjust the amount of heat they absorb from the sun. (Dark surfaces absorb more of the sun's rays than lighter surfaces.)

Body Basics: Some reptiles adjust the position of their bodies to heat up or cool down. For example, marine iguanas press their bodies against warm rock to warm up after a cold swim. If they get too warm, they raise their bodies away from the hot surface and cool off in the breeze.

Water Dwellers: Turtles, frogs, and alligators may warm up in shallow water that has been heated by the sun. To cool off, they can move to deeper, colder water.

Herps Around the World

Put together a puzzle of the world using reptile and amphibian clues.

Objectives:
Name some reptiles and amphibians and describe the habitats they live in. Point out the continents where these herps are found on a world map.

Ages:
Intermediate and Advanced

Materials:
- copies of page 18
- copies of the clues on page 14
- pencils
- paper
- world map
- scissors
- glue or tape
- construction paper
- chalkboard or easel paper

Subjects:
Science and Geography

Reptiles and amphibians live in a variety of habitats, from the Arctic Circle to the Cape of Good Hope. By putting together a puzzle of the world your kids can sharpen their geography skills while they learn about herps from around the world.

First pass out copies of page 18 and the clues on page 14. Tell the kids that by using the sets of clues, they can unscramble the puzzle pieces on the Copycat Page and form a map of the world. Explain that the shaded areas indicate land masses and the unshaded areas represent areas of water.

Point out the pictures of the reptiles and amphibians on the puzzle pieces and explain that the number next to each animal's picture corresponds to one of the clue sets on their clue sheets. Each set of clues includes the name of the animal, where it lives, and some other interesting facts about it. Tell the kids that they should carefully read these clues, not only to put the puzzle together, but also because they will need to know the information later. Also point out that they shouldn't follow the numbers to put the puzzle together, because the numbers are not in order on the map.

Now have the kids cut apart the puzzle pieces along the dashed lines and try to arrange them. (Bring out a world map for the kids to refer to as they put the puzzle pieces together.) Pass out construction paper and tape or glue. When the kids have figured out how the pieces fit together, they can tape or glue the completed maps to the construction paper.

After the kids have finished assembling their maps, go over the reptiles and amphibians that live in each area. Then have them put their maps and clue sheets aside and give each person a piece of paper and a pencil. Explain that they'll be answering questions about the animals on their maps. (You can either read the questions aloud or give each person a copy of the quiz.) List the names of the reptiles and amphibians from the clue sheet on a chalkboard or sheet of easel paper to help the kids answer the questions. After the herp quiz, go over the answers listed in parentheses.

Indian rock python

A QUICK HERP QUIZ

1. True or false: Some reptiles can live longer than people can. (True. For example, tuataras can live more than 120 years.)
2. Name two types of herps that don't have legs as adults. (caecilians and snakes)
3. Name the herp on the list that lives the farthest north. (European adder)
4. Name a reptile on the list that eats seaweed. (marine iguana)
5. True or false: Some frogs eat other frogs, mice, and rats. (True. The Brazilian horned frog is an example of a frog that eats these animals.)
6. Name a reptile on the list that spends most of its time in trees. (Madagascar rear-fanged snake)
7. What desert-dwelling amphibian on the list survives the heat by burrowing

for long periods of time? (Couch's spadefoot toad)

8. Which amphibian on the list doesn't have lungs as an adult? (dusky salamander)

9. Name a reptile on the list that spends its entire life in water. (blue-banded sea snake)

10. True or false: The world's largest amphibian is shorter than a yardstick. (False. The Japanese giant sala- mander can grow to be five feet [1.5 m] long.)

11. Name a European amphibian that is blind. (olm)

12. Which reptile on the list got its name because it has a flattened shell? (pancake tortoise)

13. Which reptile has a spine you can see through its skin? (web-footed gecko)

14. What does a flying squirrel have in common with a flying dragon? (neither can fly, but both can glide)

HERPS AROUND THE WORLD

1. **Couch's spadefoot toad**
   - lives in deserts
   - burrows into ground to escape summer heat
   - can remain in burrows for up to two years
   - found in the southwestern United States

2. **European adder**
   - lives in forested areas in Europe and Asia
   - can survive as far north as the Arctic Circle
   - hibernates underground during the winter

flying dragon

3. **Japanese giant salamander**
   - lives in mountain streams in Japan
   - largest amphibian in the world—may grow to be more than 5 ft (1.5 m) long
   - may live for 50 years in captivity

4. **Pancake tortoise**
   - lives in East African countries of Kenya and Tanzania
   - shell is somewhat flexible and flattened
   - can wedge itself between rocks so that predators can't pull it out

5. **Blue-banded sea snake**
   - flattened tail helps it swim
   - gives birth to live young
   - spends entire life in warm oceans from the Persian Gulf to Japan and New Guinea
   - eats fish that it paralyzes with venom

6. **Madagascar rear-fanged snake**
   - found only on the island of Madagascar
   - lives in trees
   - probably eats mostly lizards that it poisons with venom

7. **Olm**
   - lives in underground pools and streams
   - remains in larval stage for entire life
   - skin is pale
   - is blind
   - found in Yugoslavia and Italy

8. **Brazilian horned frog**
   - lives in rain forests in Brazil
   - eats mostly other frogs; also eats mice, rats, and other animals that it catches in its huge mouth

9. **Web-footed gecko (GEK-oh)**
   - lives in the Namib Desert in southwestern Africa
   - stays in burrows during the day to keep cool and hunts only at night
   - webbed feet help it walk on desert sand and dig burrows
   - skin is so thin that you can see its spine and some internal organs

10. **Dusky salamander**
    - lives near streams
    - adults have no lungs—instead they get the oxygen they need through their skin and mouth lining
    - found in eastern North America

11. **Marine iguana (ih-GWA-nuh)**
    - can dive to depths of 50 ft (15 m)
    - feeds on seaweed
    - flattened tail helps it swim
    - lives on rocky shores of the Galapagos Islands, a group of islands on the equator near the west coast of South America

12. **Panamanian caecilian (see-SIL-ee-an)**
    - lives in Panama
    - has no legs
    - lives in burrows
    - eats mainly insects and earthworms

13. **Flying dragon**
    - lives in forests in Malaysia and other countries in Southeast Asia
    - can glide from tree to tree on large flaps of skin that stretch along its body between its front and hind legs

14. **Tuatara (TOO-ah-TAH-rah)**
    - lives on islands off the coast of New Zealand
    - scientists think it can live for 120 years
    - lives in burrows made by seabirds—sometimes while the birds are still living there

CAST OF CHARACTERS

Narrator: Fergie Frog

The Amphibians
Chairperson: Cecilia
  Caecilian
J.T. Toad
Betty Bullfrog
Salamander Sal
Sammy Spadefoot Toad

The Reptiles
Bob "Boom Boom" Boa
Gary Gecko
Irene Iguana
Carla Chameleon
Tyrone Turtle
Allie Alligator
Terence Tuatara

Fergie Frog: Amphibians and reptiles from all over the world have gathered to discuss an important issue. They're sick and tired of being considered creepy, crawly, and unimportant animals by people. Let's listen in:

Cecilia Caecilian: As chairperson, I now call to order the first meeting of S.A.R.A. (Society for the Advancement of Reptiles and Amphibians). We all know why we're here, right?

J. T. Toad: We're going to show humans that we're important animals and worth learning about!

Bob "Boom Boom" Boa: Yeah, let's put the squeeze on those silly humans! (cheers from the crowd)

Cecilia: Order, order! (pounds on table) Does anyone here have some *serious* suggestions for what we should teach people?

Betty Bullfrog: I have one! Let's tell them what it's like to be cold-blooded.

Tyrone Turtle: That's a good idea, Betty. Cold-blooded animals like us spend a lot of time looking for places where we won't get too hot or too cold. But we don't need as much food as warm-blooded animals. So we don't have to eat as much as mammals and birds.

Betty: That's for sure! Those mammals never stop looking for food. Why, I bet Sylvester the Shrew hasn't ever taken a break to sit in the sun—he's *always* running around looking for insects and salamanders to eat.
(amphibians gasp—"How horrible!")

Gary Gecko: Hey, I think this skin thing is really important. People get grossed out because some of us shed our skin all at once and then eat it. Well, don't they know that they shed tiny pieces of skin *every* day?

Irene Iguana: Personally, I think iguana skin tastes great—and it's full of protein too!

Salamander Sal: Well, I have a complaint. I'm pretty sick of being called a lizard. Lizards are OK, but I'm an *amphibian*. I think we should make it clear that we salamanders are *not* reptiles like the lizards are.
(cheers from the amphibians)

Carla Chameleon: I'm *soooo* confused! What *is* the difference between reptiles and amphibians?

Tyrone: Boy, Carla, sometimes I think you have the IQ of an earthworm. There are some *big* differences!

Allie Alligator: For one thing, most amphibians have smooth, moist skin, unlike us reptiles. Special glands in their skin keep them slimy. And other glands make them taste bad to predators.

Boom Boom: You aren't kidding! Have you ever tasted a toad? Yuk!

Sal: And the eggs that amphibians lay don't have shells. We lay our eggs in water, which keeps them from drying out. At least, that's what most of us do.

Gary: So that's why so many of you amphibians live in wet places!

Irene: We reptiles have dry, scaly skin. And since our eggs have shells, we can lay them on land—and unless it gets too hot, they won't dry out.

Sammy Spadefoot: Wait a minute! I'm an amphibian, but my skin isn't moist—it's bumpy and dry. And I live in the desert!

Betty: That's right, Sammy. There are some exceptions. You have a lot of neat tricks for staying alive in the desert, like burrowing three feet under the ground before the hot summer season hits.

Tyrone: And that's another thing that people should know—there are a lot of unusual reptiles and amphibians in the world!

Sal: Hold on—don't forget the one thing that makes most of us amphibians *really* different—METAMORPHOSIS!

(amphibians say "Yeah!")

Tyrone: Wow, I sure would have felt silly if we forgot that one!

Sal: Many of us amphibians hatch from eggs laid in water. Then we go through metamorphosis and become adults. After that, many of us spend a lot of time on land.

Allie: Most reptiles also hatch from eggs—but our eggs are laid on land. And unlike most of you amphibians we don't go through metamorphosis.

Cecilia: Well, now that we've talked about the differences between amphibians and reptiles—what else do we think humans should know?

Boom Boom: That they'd better watch out for toads—they give you warts!

(reptiles laugh)

J. T. Toad: That's not true, and you know it, you dry, scaly-skinned creep!

(reptiles and amphibians start arguing)

Fergie: Terence Tuatara, more than 100 years old, stands up. The crowd quiets down.

Terence Tuatara (in a shaky, old voice): I've been alive for more years than most of you put together. I'm a reptile and I'm also proud to be a herp. There are lots of important things about both amphibians *and* reptiles that we can teach people. For example, Carla Chameleon can change the color of her skin in less than a minute. Can a person do that?

Carla: No way!

Terence: Right. And some snakes, lizards, and even toads like Sammy Spadefoot can survive in the desert where temperatures can be over 130 degrees and it's tough to find food and water.

Sammy: I hung out in my burrow for two years during the last big drought—bet a human couldn't stay alive in the desert for more than a week!

(crowd cheers for Sammy)

Terence: Before I sit down, I want to make one thing perfectly clear to you young, upstart reptiles—without amphibians, you wouldn't be here today.

(reptiles grumble and mumble)

Gary: What do you mean?

J. T. Toad: He means that millions of years ago we amphibians were the first vertebrates to leave the water and live part of our lives on the land!

(cheers from the amphibians)

Carla: And reptiles evolved from amphibians and became the first vertebrates to live away from water. And then birds and mammals evolved from reptiles.

Terence: Yep, J. T. and Carla are right. Just remember—amphibians *and* reptiles are both ancient and important groups of animals!

(Terence sits down)

Cecilia: Thanks, Terence. I think all of us here have learned a lot. So let's get out there and teach those people a thing or two! The first meeting of S.A.R.A. is over!

(everyone cheers)

THE END

RANGER RICK'S NATURESCOPE: LET'S HEAR IT FOR HERPS!

(See *Herps on Stage*—p 9)

COPYCAT PAGE

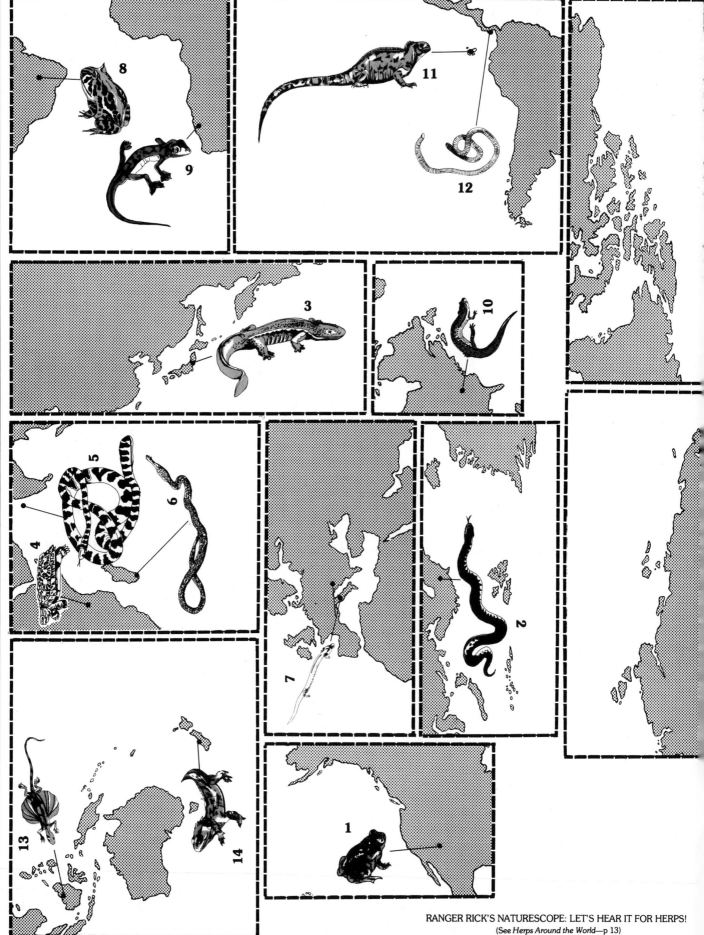

AMPHIBIANS

Compared with other vertebrates, amphibians tend to be overlooked. Why? Maybe it's because they aren't "warm and fuzzy" like mammals. Or maybe it's because they don't evoke the fascination, fear, and respect in people that reptiles often inspire. Or it could be because they lack the sporting appeal of fish or the enjoyment that comes from watching birds. But whatever the reason, they deserve a closer look.

In many ways amphibians are unique, with adaptations that are either rare or nonexistent elsewhere in the animal kingdom. And the diversity amphibians show in certain aspects of their lives, such as whether or not they care for their young and how they go about doing it, surpasses that of most other classes of animals. (See "Far-Out Frogs" on page 29 for some incredible examples of how amphibians care for their young.) Obviously, there's more to the amphibians than their humble image reveals.

WHO ARE THE AMPHIBIANS?

As we mentioned in "Sorting It All Out" on page 3, the amphibians include three groups: the salamanders, the frogs, and the caecilians (see-SIL-ee-ans). A combination of factors, such as cold-bloodedness, moist skin, and eggs without shells, characterizes these three kinds of animals as amphibians. Here's a more in-depth look at each group:

SALAMANDER SECRETS

Lizard Look-Alikes: Some people mistake salamanders for the reptiles called lizards. At first glance, some salamanders do look quite a bit like small lizards. But their physiologies, behaviors, and certain other characteristics are very unlizardlike. For example, salamanders don't have claws on their toes or scaly skin, as lizards do. And most live in temperate climates, either in cool, moist areas on land or in ponds, streams, or other bodies of water. Many lizards, on the other hand, live in drier habitats, and their distribution includes more tropical areas.

Hidden Abundance: Salamanders are usually small and quiet, and they pretty much keep to themselves. Because of this, the high number of these amphibians in certain areas can be surprising. In some forests, for example, scientists estimate that there are far more salamanders than mammals and birds put together. But unless you actively searched for them, you'd never know so many of them were there.

Nighttime Prowlers: One reason salamanders tend to be inconspicuous is that they usually stay put during the day. They rest under layers of dead leaves and other vegetation or under rocks in creeks to avoid the drying heat of the sun. But at night many salamanders come out of their hiding places. They hunt in the darkness, using their keen sense of smell and vision to help them find worms, insects, crustaceans, and other prey.

AMPHIBIANS THAT BURROW—THE CAECILIANS

"Worms" with Backbones: Not many people have heard of caecilians. These little-known tropical amphibians look, and to some extent act, like earthworms. A few are completely aquatic, but most caecilians spend their time on land, in burrows that they dig with their bullet-shaped heads. *(continued next page)*

Underground Hunters: In their underground tunnels caecilians hunt for termites, earthworms, and other small animals. Some of the larger caecilians, which can grow to five feet (1.5 m) long, also eat larger animals such as lizards. Scientists think that a strong sense of smell helps caecilians find their prey. Their "seismic" sense of hearing may also help out. (Caecilians' ears are probably very sensitive to vibrations in the ground but not to sound waves traveling through air.)

A Link With the Past?: We pointed out in chapter one that amphibians, unlike reptiles, don't have scaly skin—but caecilians are an exception. Many species have bony scales embedded in their skin, although these scales are more like those of fish than those of reptiles. Scientists aren't sure what the function of caecilians' scales are, but many think they may be a carry-over from the animals' "fishy" ancestry.

FINDING OUT ABOUT FROGS AND TOADS

Close Cousins: One of the most commonly asked questions about this group of amphibians is, "What's the difference between a frog and a toad?" Most people use the word "frog" to refer to the members of this group with smooth skin that spend the majority of their time in or near water. And most use the word "toad" to refer to the warty, chubby-looking ones that tend to spend more time away from water. But these aren't scientific groupings. They're just common names. And scientists usually refer to all members of this group as "frogs."

Conspicuous Callers: Accounting for nearly 85% of all amphibians, frogs are the extroverts in the group. Far from being reclusive and secretive, many frogs make their presence known with loud, distinctive calls. The males do most of the calling, often creating resonating chambers for their calls by inflating one or more vocal sacs with air. The most frequently made calls are the males' mating calls during the breeding season. But males and females make several other kinds of calls too. (For more about frog calls, see "Call of the Wild" on page 26.)

Here, There, and Everywhere: At certain times of the year, you can hear frogs calling throughout the night almost anywhere there's standing or slow-moving fresh water. From mountains to rain forests to prairies, just about every type of habitat is home to at least one type of frog. And some, such as certain species of spadefoot toads, even live in deserts.

From Vegetarian to Carnivore: Like salamanders and caecilians, adult frogs are carnivorous. Almost any small animals that move—insects, earthworms, fish, and even an occasional bird, snake, turtle, or mouse—are fair game if a frog can catch them. But unlike other amphibians, most frogs don't start out as meat eaters. Before they undergo metamorphosis, they eat mainly bacteria and algae. (A frog's intestines "shrink" to as little as 15% of their original length as the *tadpole,* or young frog, undergoes metamorphosis. The adult's shorter intestines are adapted to digesting animal food rather than the plant food the frog ate when it was a tadpole.)

CHANGE OF LIFE

A process that changes a plant-eating, aquatic animal with a long gut into a meat-eating, semi-terrestrial animal with a short one deserves special attention. Not all amphibians go through metamorphosis—some, for example, hatch from their eggs as miniature versions of the adults. But these *direct developers,* as they're called, are in the minority.

Encased in Jelly: Although metamorphosis is most striking in the frogs (compare a tadpole to an adult frog), this "change of life" occurs in the same basic sequence in all three groups of amphibians. First, of course, comes the egg. Most egg-laying

bullfrog   Leonard Lee Rue III

amphibians lay their eggs in water—in shallow ponds, marshes, swamps, ditches, or even (depending on the species) in tiny puddles of water that have collected among the leaves at the base of certain plants.

An egg is rarely "alone" in its watery world: Most amphibians lay dozens or even thousands of eggs at a time. The eggs usually form either big clumps, as with some salamanders and frogs, or long strands, as with other frogs. (Not all amphibians lay eggs, though. For example, a few salamanders and frogs, as well as many caecilians, give birth to live young.)

Each amphibian egg is covered with a clear or translucent "jelly" that helps protect the developing embryo. The embryo itself is a small cluster of cells in the middle of the jelly. It develops over a period of as little as one to two days or as long as several months, then hatches into the next phase of its life.

Life as a Larva: Once it hatches, a young amphibian, or *larva,* spends most of its time feeding and growing. The rate at which it grows and the length of time it spends as a larva depends on the species as well as on conditions such as food availability and the temperature of the water. (The less food there is and the cooler the water temperature, the longer the period before metamorphosis takes place.) Some amphibians, such as bullfrogs, may not go through metamorphosis for a year or more after hatching—even with plenty of food and optimal water temperatures. But others are quick-change artists. Some spadefoot toads, for example, can metamorphose into an adult about two weeks after hatching.

On the other hand, some salamanders never go completely through metamorphosis. They eventually become sexually mature, but they remain in water all their lives and never lose their gills or other larval features.

(continued next page)

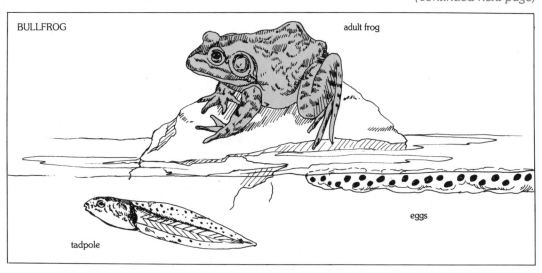

BULLFROG   adult frog

eggs

tadpole

21

Growing and Changing: Many of the changes an amphibian goes through during metamorphosis involve major alterations in physiology, anatomy, and behavior. For example, we've already discussed one of the major changes a tadpole experiences—i.e., the shortening of its intestines. Another change, which takes place not only in tadpoles but also in most salamander and caecilian larvae, is the replacement of gills with lungs.

In some young amphibians, such as tadpoles, a major revamping of the body shape and form occurs along with changes inside the body. For example, back legs and front legs grow, the tail shrinks and finally disappears as it's absorbed into the body, and the mouth expands from a small hole to a large opening capable of swallowing large insects and other food. These major changes reflect the fact that life on land as an adult requires different adaptations from life in the water as a larva.

STAYING ALIVE

"Beings with a double life." That's the definition of *amphibios*, the Greek word from which the word *amphibian* developed. It's a fitting definition for a group that has taken to the land and yet remains tied to the water.

The "double life" that amphibians lead has resulted in a lot of interesting adaptations. Some of these adaptations reflect the demands of life on land, others reflect the demands of an aquatic existence, and still others are useful in both kinds of habitats.

Slime and Poison: Some people mistakenly describe snakes and other reptiles as slimy—but it's the amphibians that can claim credit for this trait. The slime, or *mucus,* comes from glands in an amphibian's skin, and its function is to keep the skin moist—an important job that facilitates respiration. In aquatic species, mucus also helps to control the amount of water that passes into the skin.

Besides mucous glands, amphibians also have poison glands in their skin. In most cases the poison these glands produce is no more than a foul-tasting irritant that discourages predators. But some species also produce powerful toxins that can easily kill enemies—including people.

Colors That Communicate: The ability to produce a strong poison often goes hand in hand with another characteristic: bright colors that warn a would-be predator to stay away. (Many predators learn to avoid brightly colored amphibians after grabbing a poisonous one in their mouth and spitting it out.) Using bright colors to advertise toxicity isn't restricted to the amphibians—many insects, fish, reptiles, and other animals use the same strategy—but some of the most striking examples are found among the frogs and salamanders. The tropical rain forests of Central and South America, for example, are home to dozens of species of dart-poison frogs, most of which are splashed with nearly incandescent shades of red, yellow, blue, and/or other colors. And certain non-poisonous frogs take advantage of their poisonous peers by mimicking their colors and patterns.

Colors That Camouflage: Another strategy for staying alive is using color to camouflage. As with most other kinds of animals, a lot of the amphibians blend in with their surroundings. Aquatic frogs are often green like the water plants they live among, for example, and other frogs and terrestrial salamanders are often dark like the leaves of their forest-floor homes. A few amphibians also have leaflike projections on their bodies, helping them blend in even more.

Froggie Sing-Along

Discuss the changes a frog goes through from egg to adult and then sing a song about frog development.

Objectives:
Explain the life cycle of a frog. Describe the changes a frog goes through from egg to adult.

Ages:
Primary

Materials:
- *easel paper*
- *picture of a bullfrog*
- *green felt*
- *scissors*
- *Velcro fasteners*
- *movable animal eyes (available at craft stores)*
- *glue*
- *clothespins*
- *cotton balls or other stuffing material*
- *copy of the pattern pieces provided in the activity*

Subjects:
Science and Music

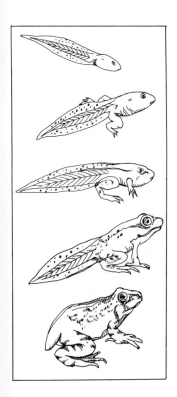

Here's a fun way to teach the kids in your group about the "double life" frogs lead. Before you get started, copy the diagram in the margin onto a sheet of easel paper. (You'll be using this diagram later.) Then copy the diagram on page 21 onto another sheet of easel paper and hang it where all the kids can see it.

Begin by showing the kids a picture of a bullfrog. Then, using the information under "Bullfrog Basics" on the next page, discuss the bullfrog's life cycle. Point to the egg mass, tadpole, and adult drawings you copied earlier as you discuss each stage. Afterward have the kids describe how each stage looks different from the others.

Now hang the other diagram where all the kids can see it. Explain that it shows what a tadpole looks like as it grows and changes into a frog. What changes do the kids notice in the tadpole as it becomes a frog? (the tail gets shorter and eventually disappears, the back legs and then front ones appear, the mouth gets much bigger, and so on) To give the kids a close-up look at some live tadpoles, you might want to take a trip to a local pond. (See "Watchers at the Pond" on page 30 for more about observing amphibian eggs and larvae in the wild.)

Next tell the kids that in addition to the differences they can see between the frog and the tadpole, the two are very different from each other on the inside too. For one thing, the frog breathes with lungs instead of gills. And the frog has different mouthparts and internal organs (its diet has changed from plants to animals).

After your discussion, have the kids form a circle. Then tell them they're going to sing a song about a bullfrog tadpole that hatches from an egg and slowly changes into a frog. First go over the words and movements and then let the kids perform!

FROGGIE GROWS UP

SONG

(Sing to the tune of "Froggie Went a-Courtin'.")

SONG	MOVEMENTS
Froggie was a-floatin' in a big ol' pond, uh-huh, uh-huh. Froggie was a-floatin' in a big ol' pond, uh-huh, uh-huh. He was one black spot in a jelly glob; One small egg in a great big blob, uh-huh, uh-huh, uh-huh.	Make wave motions with hands. Hold forefingers and thumbs together to show egg.
Soon froggie was a-swimmin' on his own, uh-huh, uh-huh. Soon froggie was a-swimmin' on his own, uh-huh, uh-huh. His fast-moving tail helped him get around. And he munched on tiny plants he found, uh-huh, uh-huh, uh-huh.	Make a tail by placing palms together behind back. Wiggle tail back and forth to swim.
And froggie was a-changin' day by day, uh-huh, uh-huh. And froggie was a-changin' day by day, uh-huh, uh-huh. First he got back legs and then front ones too. And he lost his tail and his lungs grew, uh-huh, uh-huh, uh-huh.	Hold a leg up and wiggle it, then wiggle both arms.
Now froggie is a-hoppin' on the land, uh-huh, uh-huh. Now froggie is a-hoppin' on the land, uh-huh, uh-huh. His long, sticky tongue helps him catch his prey, As he feeds on bugs and worms all day, uh-huh, uh-huh, uh-huh.	Hop in place. Stick out tongue and quickly pull it back in.

BULLFROG BASICS

Eggs—As far as scientists know, bullfrogs lay more eggs at one time than any other frog. (Some females lay over 20,000 eggs!) They lay their eggs in still, shallow water from May to July. (In areas that stay warm most of the year they lay eggs from February to October.) The eggs are laid together in a big clump, or *egg mass,* that floats near the surface of the water. Like other frogs' eggs, bullfrogs' eggs are covered with a jellylike substance that helps protect them. As the eggs are laid, the jelly soaks up water and begins to swell. Sometimes the swollen egg masses are huge—covering as much as five square feet (1.5 m²).

Tadpoles—Bullfrog tadpoles are olive-green. They feed mostly on algae that they scrape from rocks, large plants, and other surfaces in the water, and they may grow to be over four inches (10 cm) long. In parts of Louisiana and other areas in the South, the tadpoles complete metamorphosis as early as late summer. But in many other areas, they remain tadpoles until the following spring. And in northern areas, such as Maine, they usually don't complete metamorphosis until the spring after that—almost two years after they hatched from their eggs.

Adults—Bullfrogs are the largest frogs in North America. They may be eight inches (20 cm) long and they can weigh over a pound (450 g). They usually live along the banks of ponds, lakes, and slow-moving streams. And they feed on all kinds of animals including insects, other frogs, crayfish, small fish, and even small birds and snakes.

Diagram 1

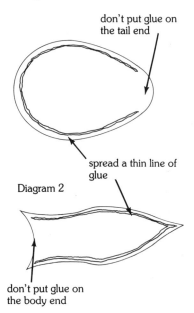

don't put glue on the tail end

spread a thin line of glue

Diagram 2

don't put glue on the body end

Diagram 3

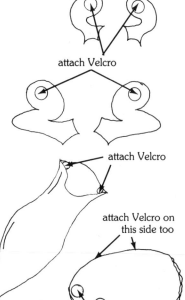

attach Velcro

attach Velcro

attach Velcro on this side too

attach Velcro

BRANCHING OUT: METAMORPHOSIS MAGIC

As a review, make this tadpole craft and have the kids tell you how to change it into a frog (see step 7). If you're working with older kids you can even let them make their own "tad-frogs."

HOW TO MAKE A TAD-FROG

1. Enlarge and trace two copies of each of the pattern pieces shown below onto a piece of green felt. Cut out all eight pieces.
2. Spread a thin line of glue around the edge of one body piece as shown in diagram 1. (Be sure to keep the tail end free of glue!) Then carefully lay the second body piece on top and let dry. (You may want to put a book or other heavy object on top of the frog's body while it dries.)

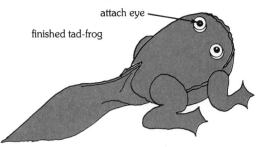

attach eye

finished tad-frog

3. When the glue has dried, stuff the frog's body with cotton balls or other stuffing. Then glue the open end closed. (Use clothespins to hold the ends together while the glue dries.)
4. Spread a thin line of glue around the edge of one of the tail pieces as shown in diagram 2. (Be sure to keep the body end free of glue!) Then carefully lay the second tail piece on top and let dry.
5. Glue one half of a Velcro fastener to each of the 12 places marked in diagram 3 and let dry. You'll need lots of glue! *Note:* Velcro comes in two parts: One half is covered with hooks and the other half is covered with fuzzy hairs. Be sure you glue the same side of the Velcro to each spot marked on the body and the other halves to the legs and tail.
6. Glue on the eyes and let dry.
7. Attach the tail to make a tadpole. Then turn the tadpole into a frog! (First attach the back legs, then the front legs, and then remove the tail.)

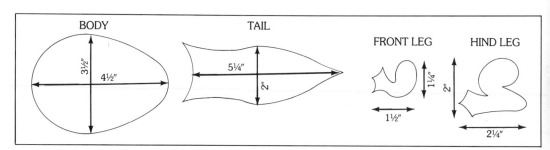

BODY	TAIL	FRONT LEG	HIND LEG
3½" 4½"	5¼" 2"	1¼" 1½"	2" 2¼"

Built to Survive!

Take a close-up look at the adaptations of a frog and a salamander.

Objective:
Describe several characteristics that help some amphibians survive.

Ages:
Primary

Materials:
- copies of pages 33 and 34
- large sheets of construction paper
- glue
- scissors
- pictures of gray tree frogs, mudpuppies, and other amphibians

Subject:
Science

Have your kids focus on two amphibians—gray tree frogs and mudpuppies—to learn about some of the adaptations that help amphibians stay alive.

Begin by explaining the concept of adaptation to the kids. Explain that all living things have special features, or *adaptations,* that help them survive. For example, a giraffe's long neck helps it reach the treetop leaves that it eats. A lion's sharp claws and teeth help it catch and kill its prey. And a duck's webbed feet help it swim.

Now pass out copies of page 34 to the kids. Explain that both of the animals shown on the page are amphibians. (You may want to use the background information on pages 19-22 to discuss the characteristics of amphibians. See "Hands-On Herps" on page 7 for more about amphibian characteristics. You can also show them pictures of different kinds of amphibians.) Have the kids look at the pictures on the Copycat Page and describe what type of habitat each one of the animals lives in. (mudpuppies live in rivers, streams, ponds, and lakes; gray tree frogs spend most of their time in trees) Then tell them that, like other living things, these two amphibians have special features that help them survive where they live. The kids will be finding out about these features.

Pass out scissors, glue, and two sheets of construction paper to each child. Have them cut apart the pictures on their Copycat Pages and glue each one to the middle of a separate piece of construction paper. Now pass out copies of page 33. Explain that all of the pictures on this page show close-ups of parts of either the mudpuppy or the gray tree frog. Have the kids cut the pictures apart and put them in a pile, in order from "A" to "G." ("A" should be on the top of the pile.)

Now have the kids look at picture A. Ask them which amphibian this part is from and what part of the body it is. (gray tree frog's legs) Then, using the information under "Prime Parts" on the next page, discuss with the kids how a gray tree frog's legs help it survive in the trees. Afterward have them glue picture A beside the gray tree frog and draw a line from it to the frog's legs. Next have the kids look at picture B. Again have them find which animal the part is from (gray tree frog's toes) and then use the information on the next page to talk about how this special feature helps the animal survive. Afterward they can glue picture B in place, draw a line connecting it with the frog's toes, and move on to picture C.

When you've finished talking about all of the pictures, review each amphibian with the kids. (See the information under "Facts About Tree Frogs and Mudpuppies" on the next page.) You might also want to mention that both of these amphibians have skin colors and patterns that help them blend into the background. A gray tree frog's skin can even change color to match the color of the leaves or bark it's sitting on.

Then tell them that these animals have a lot in common with other kinds of frogs and salamanders. Show them pictures of other frogs and salamanders and have the kids point out similarities and differences.
(continued next page)

Alvin E. Staffan   gray tree frog

PRIME PARTS

A. Long Legs: Like many frogs, gray tree frogs have long, strong hind legs for jumping and climbing. They can leap more than 2½ feet (75 cm) in a single jump! These legs help them catch food and escape predators.

B. Gripping Toes: At the ends of their toes, gray tree frogs (and most other tree frogs) have broad discs that act like suction cups to help them get a good grip on leaves, branches, and other objects. These discs also secrete a sticky substance that works like glue to help the frog hold on.

C. Thick, Flat Tail: Like many other salamanders that live in the water, mudpuppies have a thick tail that's flattened sideways. The mudpuppy swims by moving its tail from side to side.

D. Feathery Gills: With its large, feathery gills, a mudpuppy can get oxygen directly from the water. And, like most other amphibians, mudpuppies can also absorb oxygen through their skin. In water without much oxygen, mudpuppies swim to the surface of the water and use their lungs to breathe air.

E. "Eagle" Eyes: Like most other frogs, gray tree frogs have large eyes that stick up on either side of their head. With its eyes a gray tree frog can watch for prey and predators in all directions at once.

F. Outside Eardrums: The circular piece of skin located behind each of the tree frog's eyes is an eardrum, or *tympanum*. A gray tree frog hears when sound waves strike its tympanum. Hearing

is especially important for gray tree frogs during the breeding season when the males call to attract females.

G. Salamander Senses: Unlike gray tree frogs, mudpuppies have small eyes. But being able to see well is not as important for them since they live in water that is often dark and murky. Instead they rely more on their sense of smell and touch. Two nostrils on their head help them smell prey in the water. And special organs along their head, sides, and tail detect the movement of predators or prey.

FACTS ABOUT TREE FROGS AND MUDPUPPIES

Gray Tree Frogs
- grow to be a little over two inches (5 cm) long
- feed on all kinds of insects including flies, ants, and beetles, as well as spiders and other small invertebrates
- have moist bellies and legs that help them hold onto leaves and other surfaces

Mudpuppies
- grow to be 17 inches (43 cm) long
- feed on fish, frog eggs, snails, insect larvae, and other aquatic animals
- usually hide under rocks and debris during the day and come out at night to hunt

---

Call of the Wild

Talk about frog calls, create a mixed frog chorus, and take a night hike to hear frog "songs."

Objectives:
List several reasons that frogs call and explain how they call. Imitate the call of a frog.

Ages:
Primary and Intermediate

Materials:
- *recording of frog calls (see page 68 for suggestions)*

If someone asked you to imitate the sound of a frog, you probably wouldn't grunt like a pig or whistle. But some frogs make sounds just like these! And others "snore," "trill," or even "bark." Here's a way for your kids to become familiar with the sounds some amphibians make and learn why they make them. They'll also get a chance to hear (and maybe even see) some singing frogs in action. *Note:* Most scientists use the term "frog" to refer to both frogs and toads. In this activity we're using "frog" the same way. For an explanation of the differences between frogs and toads see "Close Cousins" on page 20.

Alvin E. Staffan   spring peeper

- *slips of paper*
- *record player*
- *tape recorder and blank cassette*
- *pictures of frogs with inflated vocal sacs*
- *pictures of frogs (see activity for specific species)*
- *flashlights*
- *first-aid kit*
- *insect repellent (optional)*

Subject:
Science

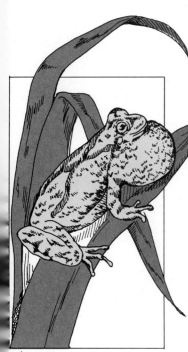
spring peeper

PART 1: FROG SONGS

Begin by having the kids imitate any frog calls they know. Then, using the information under "Making Sense of Sounds" on page 28, discuss why and how frogs call. Point out the variety of sounds these animals make—from flute-like trills to piglike grunts. Play recordings of real frogs making each of the different types of calls. (See page 68 for a listing of amphibian records, which are often available at public libraries.) And show the kids pictures of frogs with inflated vocal sacs as you explain how these sacs work. (You might also want to explain to the kids that not all frogs make sounds. For example, in many species only the males call and in others both the males and females are voiceless.)

After your discussion tell the kids that they're going to get a chance to imitate the calls of some different frogs. First copy each of the frog names listed on page 28 onto separate slips of paper and put them in a sack. Then divide the kids into five groups and have each group pick a species to imitate by drawing one of the slips of paper from the sack. Explain that all of the frogs whose names they drew are real and that they can be heard chorusing in some areas of the country.

Now show each group a picture of their frog and explain its call to them. (The calls are listed on page 28. We've also included suggestions for how to imitate the calls. These are given in parentheses after each call.) Then have the groups practice making their calls. Encourage them to give their calls clearly and not to shout them out.

Once the kids have practiced their calls, use a tape recorder to record each group one by one. Then try creating a mixed chorus by having all the groups call at once. Once again, use the tape recorder to record the kids. Afterward let the kids listen to the individual species' calls and then the mixed chorus. Can they pick their call out of the din? Can they pick out each of the other species' calls?

PART 2: OUT AT NIGHT!

Now that the kids are familiar with the reasons frogs call, take them on a night hike to hear a "live" performance! Here are some suggestions to make your trip more enjoyable:

- Ponds and wetlands are some of the best places to hear frogs calling. Be sure to visit the area during the daytime to familiarize yourself with it and to find safe spots where the kids can get close to the water's edge. Also be sure to go out the night before you take the kids to see if the frogs are calling. If there are no ponds or wetlands in your area, try a wooded area that has temporary pools in it.
- A damp, warm night in springtime or early summer is probably the best time to go out to hear frogs calling. But, depending on where you live, you may be able to hear frogs "advertising" at other times of the year as well. Check with a local nature center, zoo, natural history museum, or university de-

partment of biology, zoology, or herpetology for tips on which species you can hear at different times of the year.
- If possible, play recordings of some of the species you are likely to hear before you go on your trip.
- Wear rubber boots or old sneakers for the hike. It's easy to get your feet wet while tromping around the edges of ponds and wetlands! And depending on the time of year, you may want to bring along some "bug juice" to ward off biting insects.
- Don't forget flashlights! Once you've gotten close to some calling frogs, you can use the flashlights to get a look at them.

Safety Note: Going out at night to hear frogs calling can be a lot of fun. But it also means taking extra precautions. Be sure to get permission before visiting an area, and bring plenty of adults along to help supervise. And carry a first-aid kit with you, just in case.

MAKING SENSE OF SOUNDS

Frogs can make all kinds of sounds including clicks, whistles, grunts, and trills. Here's a run-down of the types of calls they make and why and how they make them.

WHY THEY CALL

Mating Calls: The number-one reason frogs call is to attract a mate. And almost all male frogs make mating, or *advertisement,* calls. (Female frogs don't make mating calls.) Each species has its own particular call and characteristic place (or places) to call from. For example, some frogs call from the water, some call from shore, others call from shrubs or other vegetation, and so on. Only *receptive* females—those that are ready to lay their eggs—respond to the mating calls of the males. (In some species the sound of the mating call is believed to make the females ready to breed.)

Many male frogs don't "sing" alone. Instead small numbers of them gather, often within a relatively small area, and call in a group, creating a mating *chorus.* Frog choruses are often loud and are believed to help attract females to suitable mating areas. When several different species chorus in the same general area at the same time, they create a *mixed chorus.* In many parts of the country different species mate at different times of the year, and mixed choruses may not be made up of more than

just a few species. But in Florida and some other areas in the South, there may be as many as 14 species contributing to a mixed chorus.

Territorial Calls: During the breeding season, some male frogs warn other males to stay away by giving a *territorial* call. In some species, the mating call also serves as a territorial call. In some other species, territorial calls are part of the mating call. For example, in Puerto Rico, coqui frogs have a two-note call, "co-qui." The "co" tells other male frogs to stay away, and the "qui" invites females to come closer. And some frogs have territorial calls that are completely distinct from their mating calls.

Release Calls: During the frenzy of the breeding season, adult male frogs may grab at almost anything that moves. But sometimes they grab another male or an unreceptive female. By giving a *release* call, the frogs that have been grabbed let the male know that he's wasting his time and should let go. (When frogs give release calls they also vibrate their bodies. These body vibrations may be even more important than the call in letting the male frog know he's making a mistake.)

Distress Calls: Sometimes referred to as "screams," *distress* calls are given by some frogs when they are grabbed by predators. These calls are very loud and may startle the predator into dropping the frog, allowing it to

escape. They may also warn other frogs to watch out for danger. In some species both the males and females make distress calls.

HOW THEY DO IT

Frogs make almost all of their calls with their mouth closed. (Most frogs make distress calls with their mouth open.) And most frogs make their calls using *vocal cords.* First they take air into their lungs and then they close their mouth and nostrils. Next they push the air back and forth between their lungs and mouth. As the air travels back and forth, it passes over the vocal cords and makes them vibrate, producing sound.

The speed at which air passes over a frog's vocal cords affects the type of sound the frog makes. For example, some species trill by pushing air back and forth more than 60 times per second! The size of a frog and the way its vocal cords vibrate also affect the type of sound it makes.

Many male frogs also have *vocal sacs* that resonate their calls. These sacs are stretchy pouches of skin located near the frog's mouth or neck. The male inflates his vocal sacs by pushing air through slits in the floor of his mouth. As he calls, his inflated sacs resonate the sound.

Depending on the species, a male frog may have one or two vocal sacs. When they're inflated, some vocal sacs look like balloons.

FROGS AND THEIR CALLS

Gray Tree Frog—flutelike trill (put tongue on roof of mouth and trill)
Spotted Chorus Frog—rasping trill (say "wrrank, wrrank, wrrank," trilling the Rs)
Strecker's Chorus Frog—clear, sharp whistles (give high-pitched whistle, two whistles per second)
Northern Cricket Frog—metallic, measured clicking (say "gick, gick, gick," one "gick" per second)
Great Plains Narrow-Mouthed Toad—high-pitched nasal sound (say "NEEEEEEE")

Far-Out Frogs

Discuss ways some frogs take care of their eggs and young, then take a quiz about frog parents.

Objective:
Name several frogs and describe how they help their young survive.

Ages:
Primary and Intermediate

Materials:
● *copies of page 35*
● *pencils*
● *pictures of frogs (see activity for specific species)*

Subject:
Science

Most frogs lay their eggs in the water and then abandon them. But not all frogs reproduce this way. In fact, some have pretty unbelievable strategies for taking care of their offspring. In this activity the kids in your group will find out about some of these unusual frogs and the different ways they protect their eggs and young. *Note:* Most scientists use the term "frog" to refer to both frogs and toads. In this activity we're using "frog" the same way. For an explanation of the differences between frogs and toads see "Close Cousins" on page 20.

Begin by showing the kids a picture of a bullfrog or leopard frog. (Depending on where you live, at least one of these frogs is probably found in your area.) Tell the kids that a female bullfrog or leopard frog lays thousands of eggs each year in a pool, pond, or other body of water. Tadpoles hatch from the eggs and later metamorphose into frogs.

Ask the kids what advantage there is to laying so many eggs. (Many of the eggs and tadpoles are eaten by fish, birds, aquatic insects, and other predators. By laying large numbers of eggs, these frogs increase the chances that at least a few of the tadpoles that hatch from the eggs will survive to become adults.) Can the kids think of any other animals that use this strategy? (most insects, spiders, fish, other amphibians, and so on)

Next tell the kids that even though most frogs use the same strategy as the bullfrog and leopard frog, there are some other frogs that do things quite differently. Then pass out a copy of page 35 and a pencil to each child. Explain that you are going to read a description (see next page) of how each of the frogs on the Copycat Page takes care of its eggs and/or young. The kids can then decide if the animal is real or imaginary. (You should read only the information that's in color.) If they think the amphibian really exists, the kids should circle "Yes"; otherwise they should circle "No."

Afterward tell the kids that all the frogs on the page are real and take care of their eggs and young in the ways that you described. Then go over each frog using the information printed in black on page 30. If possible, show the kids pictures of each frog as you discuss it. Tell them that predators sometimes do eat the eggs, tadpoles, and young of these "different" frogs. But because the parents guard the eggs, carry the eggs around with them, or protect them in some other way, a lower percentage get eaten. Also point out that the ways these frogs reproduce are no better than the methods used by other frogs. All animals are adapted to the places where they live and each species has developed strategies that help it survive.

(continued next page)

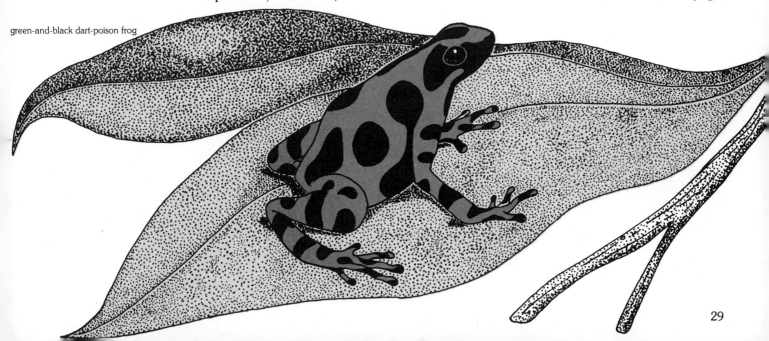

green-and-black dart-poison frog

SOME FAR-OUT FROGS

1. Suriname Toad: At breeding time, the skin on the back of this female toad becomes spongy. As she lays her eggs, the male pushes them onto her back. Then, after all 50-100 of her eggs are in place, the skin swells and covers the eggs, sealing each one in a separate pouch. The eggs develop within the tiny pouches. In about three months tiny toads pop out of their mother's back. These frogs live in parts of South America. They spend their entire lives in the water. Their dark bodies help them blend in with the mud at the bottom of the streams, rivers, and swamps where they live. Their fingertips are star-shaped and covered with tiny "hairs" that they use to comb through the water and mud searching for food.

2. Midwife Toad: As the female toad starts to lay her strings of eggs, the male pulls them out of her body and wraps them around his legs. Then he hops off to a protected place. He carries the eggs for several weeks, dunking them in water or dragging them through the dew to keep them moist. When he senses that the eggs are ready to hatch, he hops into a pond and the hatching tadpoles swim away.

Midwife toads live in Europe. At mating time, each female lays about 15-60 eggs on land. A male toad may carry eggs from more than one female at a time.

3. Green-and-Black Dart-Poison Frog: After the female lays her eggs under leaves on the ground, the male guards them. When the tadpoles hatch they wriggle onto their father's back. Then he carries them from the ground to water-filled holes in trees. Once in the water the tadpoles let go of their father and finish growing within their "treetop" nurseries. These colorful frogs live in the trees in the rain forests of Central and South America. Sometimes the father also carries the tadpoles to water-filled plants called *bromeliads* that grow in the trees, to small puddles on the ground, or to other small water-filled spots. Like most of the other kinds of dart-poison frogs, they have brightly colored skin. Their skin warns would-be predators that the frogs are poisonous.

4. Smith Frog: At mating time, the male frog builds a mud nest on the edge of a pond. Using his front feet, he pushes the mud up into a circular wall. When it's finished, the nest is about a foot (30 cm) wide with three to four inches (7.5-10 cm) of water in it. The female lays her eggs in the water within the nest. The eggs and the tadpoles that hatch from them are relatively safe from aquatic insects and other predators.

Smith frogs are tree frogs that live in parts of South America. They get their common name from the sound of the male's call: It sounds like a blacksmith's hammer striking an anvil. Like other tree frogs, smith frogs have disks on their toes and fingers that help them grip bark and leaves.

5. Glass Frog: The female frog usually lays her eggs on a leaf that hangs over a stream. She lays her eggs in a big, jelly-covered clump, and the male frog watches over them as the tadpoles develop inside. After about two weeks the tadpoles are old enough to swim and the jelly turns to liquid. One by one the tadpoles "drip" into the stream below.

Glass frogs live in rain forests in parts of Mexico and Central and South America. The adults live on the leaves of trees and shrubs, and their bright green color helps hide them from predators. The disks on their fingers and toes help them grip the bark and leaves of the trees and shrubs.

6. Darwin's Frog: After the female frog lays her eggs, the male guards them. Then, as soon as the tadpoles start to hatch, he slurps them up. The tadpoles slide from his mouth into his vocal sac. They develop inside the sac for almost three months. Then the male opens his mouth and as many as 20 little frogs crawl out.

Darwin's frogs are tiny—they're not much more than one inch (2.5 cm) long. They live mainly on the ground near streams. And they're found only in parts of Chile and Argentina.

Watchers at the Pond

Go outside to observe amphibian eggs and larvae.

Objectives:
Explain the life cycle of a frog, toad, or salamander. Describe the eggs and larvae of an amphibian.

Ages:
Primary, Intermediate, and Advanced

In many areas spring is a great time to take your group to a pond, marsh, or other wet area to get a firsthand look at amphibian eggs and larvae. Begin the activity by showing the kids pictures of adult frogs, toads, and salamanders. Then, using the information on pages 20-22 and under "Notes About Eggs and Larvae" on page 32, discuss amphibian life cycles with your group. Show them pictures of amphibian eggs and larvae.

Ask the kids to describe where amphibians lay their eggs, what the eggs look like, how the larvae are suited to their watery world, and how the larval and adult forms are different from one another. Next tell the kids that they're going to see some of the stages in amphibians' life cycles for themselves. (You may want to take the kids on a night hike to listen for male frogs calling for mates. See "Call of the Wild" on page 26 for more about frog calls.)

Materials:

- pictures of amphibian eggs, larvae, and adults
- dip nets
- plastic collecting containers
- first-aid kit
- hand lenses (optional)
- insect repellent (optional)
- clipboards or cardboard and rubber bands (optional)
- pencils (optional)
- copies of the questions on page 32 (optional)

Subject:
Science

If you're working with an older group, use the sample questions at the end of the activity to make up worksheets so the kids can record their observations of amphibian eggs and larvae. The kids can fill out a separate sheet for each different kind of egg or larva they find. (Younger kids can talk about their finds.)

Now follow the suggestions below for taking your kids on an amphibian "eggs-pedition"!

TIPS FOR THE TRIP

Getting Ready: Ponds, wetlands, woodland pools, and slow-moving streams are some of the best places to look for amphibian eggs and larvae. You may even want to visit different places to look for different kinds of eggs and larvae. Check with a local nature center for suggestions on where to go.

Before you take the kids out, visit the area and familiarize yourself with it. A dock or boardwalk that's close to the water may be an excellent place for the kids to work. If these aren't available, look for spots where the kids can safely get close to the water.

Have the kids dress appropriately for the expedition. Wearing rubber boots or old sneakers is a good idea.

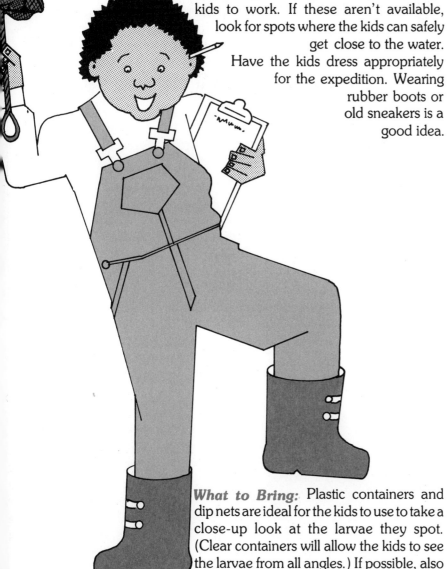

What to Bring: Plastic containers and dip nets are ideal for the kids to use to take a close-up look at the larvae they spot. (Clear containers will allow the kids to see the larvae from all angles.) If possible, also bring along hand lenses for the kids to use. And for each older child, bring several copies of the worksheets you made earlier, a clipboard, and a pencil. (If you don't have clipboards, have the kids attach their sheets to cardboard with rubber bands.)

You may also want to bring along some "bug juice" to ward off biting insects. And bring a first-aid kit, just in case.

Observing Eggs: Individual eggs and small clusters are usually harder to spot than large egg masses. Look carefully to find different kinds of eggs. And don't worry about trying to identify the eggs you find—sometimes even the experts have trouble. If the eggs are within reach, let the kids *very gently* feel them. But tell them *not* to actually pick up or disturb the eggs because it's easy to damage the protective jelly coat.

Observing Larvae: Larvae can be pretty easy to spot if they're swimming around. But also look for larvae resting on the bottom. Once the kids have observed the "free-swimming" larvae, demonstrate how to dip for them. First fill a container with water, then gently scoop up a larva with a net, trying not to stir up the bottom. (Stirring up a lot of silt can clog the larvae's gills.) Carefully release the larva into the container and let the kids take a close-up look. Then let them explore on their own to see what kinds of larvae they can catch and observe. Afterward make sure the kids return the larvae to where they were found.

Wrapping It Up: After your expedition, review the information the kids collected and compare the different eggs and larvae that they observed. (Younger kids can draw pictures of what they saw.) If you can, take the kids back several more times so they can observe how the eggs and larvae change over time.

(continued next page)

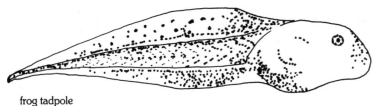
frog tadpole

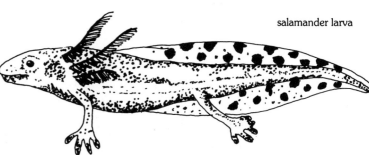
salamander larva

NOTES ABOUT EGGS AND LARVAE

Alone or in a Group—Many frogs, toads, and salamanders lay their eggs in ponds, streams, or other bodies of water. And depending on the species, they may lay their eggs in a large mass (bullfrog), in strings (American toad), in a cluster (spotted salamander), or individually (red-spotted toad). The eggs may be free-floating, attached to underwater sticks or vegetation, or stuck to the undersides of rocks or logs.

When the Time Is Right—How soon larvae hatch from the eggs and how soon they go through metamorphosis depend on the species and the temperature of the water where the eggs are laid. For example, bullfrogs usually lay their eggs in the spring. In Louisiana, bullfrog tadpoles often go through metamorphosis during their first winter. But in South Carolina they remain tadpoles for a full year. And bullfrog tadpoles in Maine usually don't metamorphose for almost two years.

QUESTIONS ABOUT EGGS

1. Draw a picture of the eggs.
2. What color are they?
3. Is anything moving inside them?
4. How big are they?
5. How do they feel?

QUESTIONS ABOUT LARVAE

1. Observe a larva for a few minutes before trying to catch one. Where does the larva spend most of its time? (on the bottom, near the surface, swimming around in the middle)
2. Describe several things you see it doing.
3. After catching a larva, draw a picture of it.
4. Describe how it moves.
5. Draw a close-up of its tail.
6. Draw a close-up of its mouth.
7. Draw a close-up of its legs, if it has any.
8. Describe the habitat where it lives.

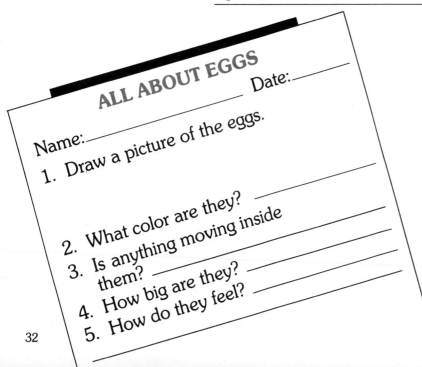

ALL ABOUT EGGS   Date:_____

Name:_____
1. Draw a picture of the eggs.

2. What color are they? _____
3. Is anything moving inside them? _____
4. How big are they? _____
5. How do they feel? _____

32

A

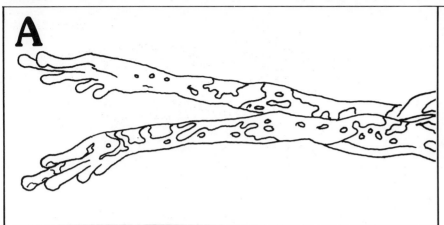

B

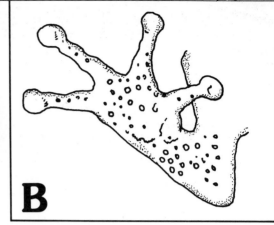

C

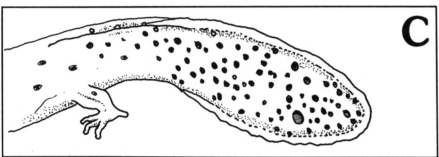

D

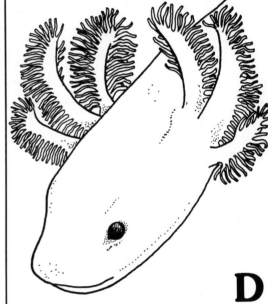

E

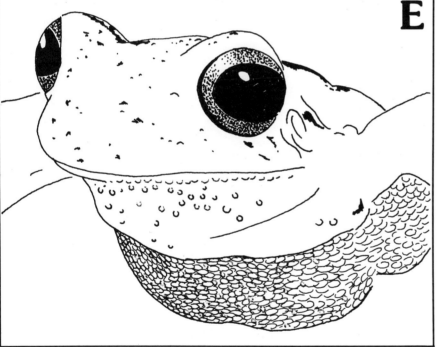

G

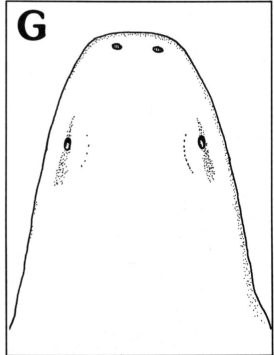

F

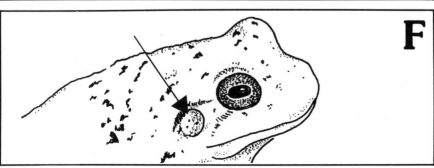

(See *Built to Survive!*—p 25)

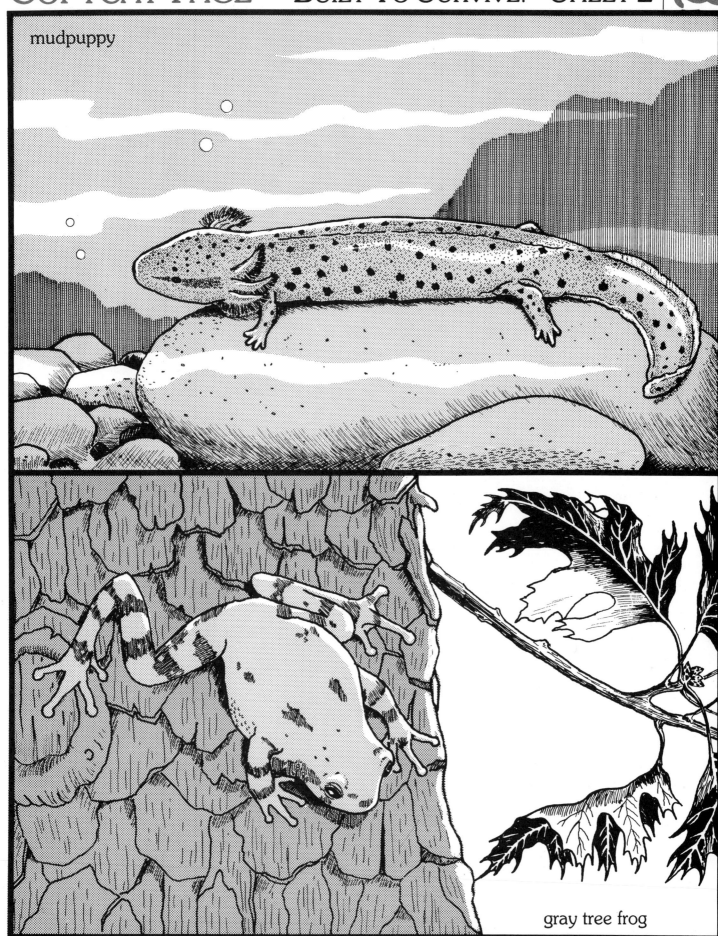

mudpuppy

gray tree frog

(See *Built to Survive!*—p 25)

COPYCAT PAGE

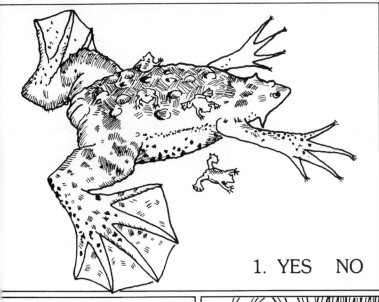

1. YES   NO

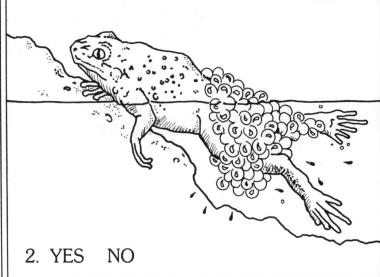

2. YES   NO

3. YES   NO

4. YES   NO

5. YES   NO

6. YES   NO

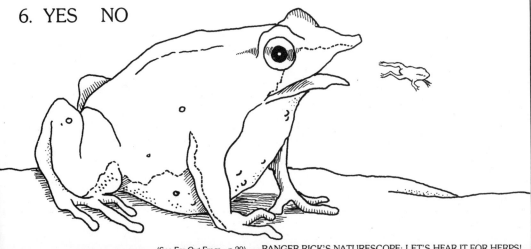

REPTILES

Reptiles are one *amazing* group of animals. There are giant snakes longer than a bus that can swallow crocodiles whole. There are bizarre turtles with fleshy skin flaps that lure fish to their death. There are three-horned lizards with turret-like eye sockets and tongues as long as their bodies. And there are sea turtles, weighing as much as a large horse, that can swim faster than you can run. And that's just the start. In this chapter, we'll take a close-up look at the characteristics of this diverse crew, which includes turtles, lizards, snakes, and crocodiles, and two lesser-known groups—the worm-lizards and the tuatara. And we'll focus on some of the amazing ways they are adapted for survival.

TAKING A LOOK AT TURTLES

There are over 200 species of turtles in the world, living on almost every continent and in most of the world's oceans. Some turtles, such as sea turtles and softshell turtles, spend almost their entire life in oceans, lakes, or rivers. Others, such as bog turtles and wood turtles, are semi-aquatic, spending their time in bogs, swamps, marshes, and other wetland areas. And many turtles, such as tortoises and box turtles, live their entire life on land. (*Note:* The term "turtle" refers to all the reptiles in this group. "Tortoise" and "terrapin" are sometimes used to refer to specific kinds of turtles.)

What Makes a Turtle a Turtle?: The most noticeable feature turtles share is a shell—the tough, armorlike covering that encloses their bodies. The shell varies from species to species, but it always consists of the same three-part structure: the *carapace,* which covers the back; the *plastron,* which covers all or part of the belly; and the *bridge,* which connects the two. Most turtle shells are covered with horny plates; others are protected by tough, leathery skin.

Turtles lay clusters of eggs in soil or sand. And they breathe with lungs, although a few may also get some oxygen through their skin and the lining of the throat.

Feeding, Turtle-Style: Like birds, turtles do not have teeth; instead they use their feet and horny beaks to rip, tear, and cut their food. (Most turtles have hard beaks, but a few, such as the matamata, have soft mouthparts.) As a group, turtles feed on a variety of foods, from insects, worms, and fish to fruit, mushrooms, and other plant material.

GETTING TO KNOW LIZARDS, SNAKES, AND WORM-LIZARDS

Together, lizards and snakes make up the largest group of reptiles. (There are roughly 3700 species of lizards and 2400 species of snakes.) Even though they don't look like "cousins," these scaly creatures are closely related. By studying fossil remains and comparing characteristics of living snakes and lizards, scientists have concluded that snakes probably evolved from an ancient line of lizards about 135 million years ago. (Worm-lizards, a small group of burrowing reptiles, are also considered part of the lizard and snake group. Although these rarely seen reptiles have characteristics of both lizards and snakes, they are different enough to make many scientists think they should be classified as a separate group.)

LOTS OF LIZARDS

When you're talking lizards, you're talking variety. Take the way they get around. Some climb trees; some glide from tree to tree; some "swim" through hot

false map turtle

snake-eyed lacertid

desert sands; a few can stand up and run on their hind legs; some can crawl upside down; some burrow into the soil; and some don't have any legs at all and slither to get around. Lizards also vary in color, size, and shape, and in the way they behave. So what makes a lizard a lizard? Here are some general lizard characteristics:

Eyes, Ears, and Legs: Like most vertebrates, many lizards have movable eyelids. And most also have external ear openings on the sides of their head. (Most lizards have good hearing, but they also rely on their sense of sight and smell to know what's going on.) And although there are a few species of legless lizards, most lizards have four legs, with five clawed toes on each foot.

Lizard Chow: Lizards usually feed on anything they can catch and swallow, which, depending on the species, can include other reptiles, insects, spiders, worms, and mammals. But some feed mainly on fruit, flowers, and leaves, and almost all vary their diet with the season.

Lizard Survival: When lizards run into trouble, each species has its own survival strategy. Some lizards nimbly scramble out of sight. Others puff up, act tough, and then run. A few stay and fight. Some "freeze." And as was mentioned in chapter one, some can change colors in a matter of seconds to match their surroundings—a great way to seem to disappear quickly.

Some lizards also use their tails as a special defense decoy. When a lizard is attacked, its tail breaks off at a special fracture joint. Often the tail keeps twitching for a few seconds, distracting the predator while the lizard makes a quick getaway. Lizards that lose their tails can slowly regenerate new ones.

Tail and Tongue Tricks: Tails are also important to lizards for other reasons. They help lizards keep their balance as they walk, swim, or run. And many lizards rely on their tails as storehouses of fat that can be used during cold weather and droughts when food is scarce.

Lizards also have well-developed tongues, and many use them to zap their food, clean their eye coverings, smell, and even scare their enemies. Some chameleons' tongues are incredibly long and can shoot out about as far as the length of their body.

Born a Lizard: Most lizards are egg-layers, usually hiding their eggs in nest cavities they dig in the soil, or under logs or rocks. But in some species, the eggs develop inside the mother's body until the embryos are well developed. The females then give birth to live young.

SIZING UP SNAKES

Snakes are missing body parts that many other animals have. For example, they don't have legs, eyelids, outside ear openings, or bladders. And instead of having a pair of lungs, many have only one. Snakes also look very different from most other animals. They have greatly elongated bodies that can twist and turn in ways that make them look like contortionists.

Moving Like a Snake: Snakes can coil, climb, and slither because they have a very flexible spine made up of 100-400 vertebrae, each of which is attached to a pair of separate, thin ribs. Most snakes move in a series of S-shaped curves, pushing themselves along using plants, rocks, sticks, and other irregularities as shove-off points.

Many snakes can also travel in almost a straight line using the wide, overlapping

Eastern green mamba

plates, or *belly scales,* on their undersides. Muscles attached to the ribs pull and lift these scales, creating a series of wavelike motions. As the scales push against rough surfaces on the ground, the snake moves forward. Many thick-bodied snakes, such as pythons, often move in this way.

Most snakes use a combination of these two methods, but some also use an accordion-type movement—especially when climbing trees. And a few desert snakes move using a complicated series of sideways body twists.

Snake Senses: Snakes have a variety of ways to sense their environment. They have fairly good "close-up" eyesight and an excellent sense of smell. Their flicking, forked tongue and a structure in the roof of their mouth called the Jacobson's organ are, in combination, responsible for their incredible ability to "smell" their environment. (For more about the Jacobson's organ, see "How Herps Smell" on page 4.)

For a long time, people thought snakes were deaf. But they can actually hear low-frequency sounds and they can feel vibrations. That's why snakes often sense your presence long before they see you.

Some snakes also have incredible sensory devices that other reptiles don't have—heat sensors located in pits on the sides of their face or on their lips. These heat sensors can detect slight differences in the amounts of radiant heat energy that animals give off. Snakes process the information to determine both the direction and distance of the objects. These heat sensors allow snakes to successfully hunt mammals, birds, and other prey in complete darkness.

Gulping Their Grub: Snakes always swallow their food whole. They can do this because they have some incredible "mouth machinery." Snakes can move their upper jaw away from their lower jaw and the left side of their lower jaw away from the right side. This expandability, due to extremely elastic muscles and ligaments in the throat and between bones in the jaw, allows snakes to swallow animals that are several times bigger than their head. Most snakes also have rows of sharp, curved teeth on each jawbone that help hold the prey and "walk" it down the throat.

Because they can eat such huge meals at one time and because they are cold-blooded, snakes don't have to eat as often as other animals. If necessary, most snakes can get away with eating just a few times per year. (For more about cold-blooded animals, see "Hot 'n' Cool Herps" on page 10.)

Meat-Eating Strategies: All snakes are meat eaters that feed on a variety of prey, including other snakes, lizards, birds, insects, worms, mammals, amphibians, and fish. Many snakes, such as boas, pythons, and rat snakes, kill their prey by constriction—squeezing so tightly that the victim can't breathe and eventually suffocates. Others, such as garter snakes and water snakes, rely on their jaws and curved teeth to keep hold of their struggling prey. And poisonous snakes, such as rattlesnakes, cottonmouths, and cobras, use venom to subdue their prey. The venom is located in sacs connected to sharp fangs. When some poisonous snakes, such as rattlesnakes, bite their prey, they jab their fangs into the prey's skin or muscle. This forces the venom to flow from the sacs through the fangs and into the animal's body. Other poisonous snakes, such as coral snakes, have shorter fangs, and their venom is injected only after several bites or as they hang on to or chew their prey.

Reproduction, Snake-Style: Most snakes lay eggs, but some give birth to live young, just as some lizards do. And like most reptiles, snakes don't care for their young after hatching. Some snakes, such as pythons, incubate their eggs by coiling their bodies around the eggs until they hatch. And a few snakes, such as the king cobra, use mud, leaves, and other materials to build a nest.

CLOSE-UP ON CROCODILIANS

Crocodiles, alligators, caimans, and gavials—the major types of crocodilians—are all semi-aquatic predators that live in warm areas around the world. And they all have the distinctive crocodilian look: a large, toothy snout, a compressed, powerful tail, and a tough, leathery hide.

As a group, crocodilians have been around for over 200 million years, having evolved from the same group of reptiles that eventually gave rise to the dinosaurs. The largest crocodilian of all time, *Deinosuchus*, was over 50 feet (15 m) long—a monster compared to crocodilians today.

Adapted to Water: Special adaptations help crocodilians hunt for food, which, depending on their species and age, could include insects, crustaceans, mollusks, fish, amphibians, reptiles, birds, and mammals. Here are just a few of their aquatic feeding tricks:

- eyes and nostrils set high on their head that allow them to see and breathe while the rest of their body is submerged in the water, out of sight
- a third eyelid, called the *nictitating membrane*, that protects their eyes underwater
- nostrils and ears that close when they dive
- a valve at the back of their mouth that closes when they dive, allowing them to catch prey without swallowing water
- a muscular, compressed tail that helps propel them through the water
- webbed feet that help them walk on mud and sand

Mounds of Heat: Like most reptiles, crocodilians are egg-layers. Their eggs look something like chicken eggs, although they are not as brittle. Some species dig shallow pits in the sand and bury their eggs. Others hide their eggs in nests of decaying vegetation and mud. Some croc mothers also protect their nests, staying around until the young hatch.

WHAT'S A TUATARA?

Most people have never heard of tuataras—lizardlike reptiles that live on about 30 small islands off the coast of New Zealand. Tuataras are the only survivors of an entire order of reptiles that evolved about 220 million years ago—about the time of the first dinosaurs.

What else is special about the tuataras? For one thing, these nocturnal burrowers have a third "eye" on top of their head, which is connected to their brain and which scientists think is sensitive to light. (Several lizards also have this "eye.") Tuatara eggs also have the longest incubation time of all the reptiles, taking about 15 months to hatch. And many of these reptiles have incredibly long life spans, living more than a century.

spectacled caiman

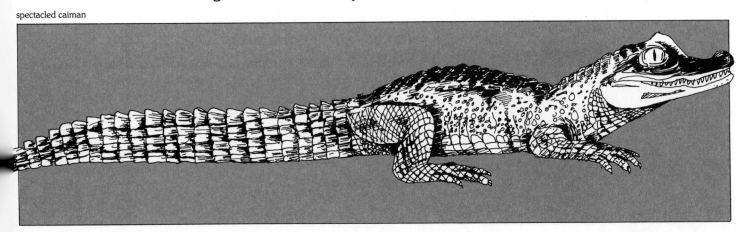

Reptile Countdown

Make a reptile number book and sing a reptile counting song.

Objectives:
Name several types of reptiles. Discuss their differences and group them according to their similarities.

Ages:
Primary

Materials:
- *copies of pages 47 and 48*
- *construction paper*
- *drawing paper*
- *scissors*
- *glue*
- *crayons or markers*
- *stapler*
- *easel paper*
- *pictures of reptiles*

Subjects:
Science and Math

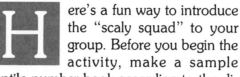

ere's a fun way to introduce the "scaly squad" to your group. Before you begin the activity, make a sample reptile number book according to the directions below.

Next pass out copies of page 47. Tell the kids that the animals on the page are all reptiles. Discuss some of the general characteristics of reptiles, using the background information on pages 36-39, and show the kids pictures of some of the reptiles on the Copycat Page.

Then tell the kids to look at the pictures on their Copycat Page and describe some of the ways the reptiles are different from each other. (For example, some have shells and others don't; some have legs, others are legless; and so on.) After your discussion, have the kids cut the reptiles apart and divide them into several small piles, putting together the ones they think are similar.

After they've finished, have the kids explain why they grouped certain animals together. Then make a chart on a sheet of easel paper to go over the main groupings of reptiles (see diagram).

Explain that scientists group these animals according to their body structure, physiology, and other characteristics. That's why some animals that look the same aren't always grouped together. For example, a tuatara looks a lot like a lizard. But scientists know that tuataras are different from lizards in several ways.

After your discussion have the kids use their reptile pictures to make a counting book and to sing a reptile song.

A NUMBER BOOK OF REPTILES

Show the sample book that you made earlier and explain to the kids that they will make their own reptile counting books. Pass out a copy of page 48, a piece of construction paper, and seven sheets of drawing paper to each child. Here's how to make a book:

1. Fold the drawing paper and construction paper in half widthwise. Insert the folded drawing paper in the construction paper to make a book with a cover. Staple the pages together, then write a title on the cover and your name on the first page (see diagram).
2. Cut apart the groups of reptile silhouettes on page 48 (cut along dashed lines).
3. Find the picture with only one silhouette. Then find the reptile from page 47 that matches it. (box turtle)
4. Open the book to the second and third pages. Glue the single box turtle silhouette on the left-hand page and write the number "1." Glue the picture of the box turtle from page 47 on the right-hand page (see diagram).
5. Find the reptile with two silhouettes and its match. (gavial) Glue and label these pictures on the next two pages of your book. Continue until you've completed the book with the 12 tuataras.

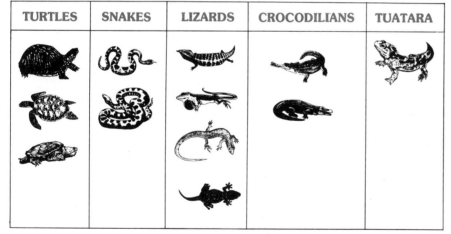

TURTLES	SNAKES	LIZARDS	CROCODILIANS	TUATARA

Sing a Song of Reptiles

After the children have finished making their number books, they can sing a special song to go along with the books. Here's how it goes, sung to the tune of "Twelve Days of Christmas":

Luise Woelflein

On the first page of reptiles
We'll get to know so well:
A box turtle in a snug shell.

On the second page of reptiles
We'll get to know so well:
Two gavials and a box turtle in a snug shell.

...and so on until the last verse:

On the twelfth page of reptiles
We'll get to know so well:
12 tuataras, 11 anacondas, 10 snapping turtles, 9 green anoles, 8 fringe-toed lizards, 7 alligators, 6 green sea turtles, 5 blue-tongued skinks, 4 rattlesnakes, 3 geckos, 2 gavials, and a box turtle in a snug shell.

To make it more fun, have the kids take turns "performing" the song. First use the information under "Meet the Reptiles" to talk about each animal. Then have the group think of a way to act out each one, based on the animal's characteristics and behavior.

Next have 12 kids come up and stand in a line or semi-circle. Each will play the role of one of the reptiles while the rest of the group sings the song. Then as a new reptile is introduced in each verse, the child whose part it is can sing and act out his or her part. By the last verse, all twelve kids will be performing their parts in turn. After they've finished, pick a new group of performers from the audience.

Meet the Reptiles

Box turtle: A kind of land turtle with a high-domed shell. It's one of the few turtles that can completely close their shell for defense—a handy trick when enemies come near.

Gavial: A needle-nosed relative of the crocodile and alligator that lives in India and other parts of Asia. It feeds almost entirely on fish, which it catches by swinging its jaws from side to side in the water.

Gecko: A lizard with special toes that enable it to cling to any surface, even upside-down. It's one of the most vocal reptiles, and has the ability to bark, shriek, chirp, or cluck, depending on the species.

Rattlesnake: Most species of this poisonous snake vibrate the "rattle" on the end of the tail as a warning. Rattlesnakes feed mostly on warm-blooded animals such as rabbits, rodents, and birds.

Blue-tongued skink: A large Australian lizard with a broad, bright blue tongue. This skink often sticks its flattened tongue way out and hisses to scare away predators.

Green sea turtle: One of several kinds of marine turtles. Sea turtles spend their lives in the ocean and females come ashore only to lay eggs. Their flippers help them swim.

Alligator: A large reptile that lives in temperate or subtropical wetlands. It has a broad snout with powerful jaws and sharp teeth.

Fringe-toed lizard: A desert-dwelling reptile with fringed feet that help it walk on loose sand. To reduce contact with the hot sand, some of these lizards often raise a front foot and opposing rear foot in unison, alternating with the other pair.

Green anole: A small lizard with a brightly colored flap of skin under the throat that fans out in threat and courtship displays. Like many other lizards, the green anole bobs its head and does "push-ups" during its displays.

Snapping turtle: A freshwater turtle with a powerful beaked jaw and strong claws. It feeds on just about anything it can find—small mammals, birds, fish, crayfish, worms, and other aquatic creatures.

Anaconda: A South American snake in the boa family that spends a lot of time in the water. It is one of the longest snakes in the world, often growing to nearly 30 feet (9 m).

Tuatara: An endangered lizardlike reptile that lives on islands off the coast of New Zealand. It can raise the spikes of skin on its back when alarmed.

Close-Up on Cobras

Take a look at snake characteristics by making a cobra flip-up.

Objectives:
Describe several characteristics of snakes. Name some of the ways a snake is adapted for survival.

Ages:
Intermediate and Advanced

Materials:
- *copies of page 49*
- *copies of the king cobra facts on page 43*
- *tracing paper*
- *cardboard*
- *paper and pencils*
- *glue*
- *raw, shelled sunflower seeds*
- *modeling clay*
- *pictures of snakes*
- *stapler*

Subjects:
Science, Language Arts, and Arts and Crafts

enlarged section of body

sunflower seeds

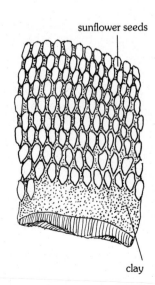

clay

There's no doubt about it: Cobras are "cool." And regardless of how kids feel about snakes in general, they're usually fascinated by cobras. You can take advantage of this fascination by having the kids make a cobra "flip-up" to learn more about the characteristics of snakes. Before getting started, make a sample cobra yourself, using the directions under "Making the Flip-Up."

Begin by showing the kids pictures of snakes and reviewing the characteristics that all reptiles share. (See pages 3-4 for more about reptilian characteristics.) If possible, take a trip to a zoo, nature center, or natural history museum to give your kids a firsthand "feel" for snakes. Let them look at a variety of snakes and note the differences and similarities they see. Afterward discuss their observations.

Next pass out copies of page 49 and the king cobra facts on page 43 to each person. Explain that the skeleton on page 49 is that of a king cobra. Then discuss the characteristics of the king cobra and snakes in general, using the completed flip-up you made earlier, the information under "Snakes, Inside and Out," and the background information on pages 37-38. Tell the kids to take notes of the discussion on a separate piece of paper. Explain that they'll be using these notes later when they make their own flip-ups.

After your discussion, pass out a pencil, piece of tracing paper, two sheets of cardboard, a lump of clay about the size of a baseball, a pile of sunflower seeds, and glue to each person. Then have the kids follow the directions below to make a cobra flip-up.

MAKING THE FLIP-UP

1. Glue the page with the cobra skeleton to one of the sheets of cardboard.
2. Lay the tracing paper over the skeleton and trace the outline of the cobra. Glue the outline to the other sheet of cardboard.
3. Spread the clay within the snake's outline, making the clay thick enough to give the cobra a three-dimensional look.
4. Starting at the tail, stick the seeds into the clay to form rows of "scales" (see diagram). Continue to make rows of scales until you reach the point where the front of the snake is raised up, showing the underside of the cobra.
5. Make the large, narrow belly scales by marking lines across the snake's underside with the tip of a pencil. Where the neck is flattened to form the hood, the scales are stretched apart. Put several seed "scales" on the sides of the hood, setting them apart from one another (see diagram).
6. Mark the eye and nostril with a pencil tip.
7. Staple the pieces of cardboard together along the top, with the clay snake on top of the skeleton.

When the kids have completed their cobra flip-ups, have them each write a paragraph about the cobra, using the fact sheet about cobras and the notes they took during the discussion. Then tell them to glue the paragraph to the back side of the top piece of cardboard so that when they lift the clay snake, they can read about it. They can also glue their cobra facts on the page with the cobra skeleton. Finally have them label the ribs, fangs, backbone or vertebrae, hood, eyes, tail, belly scales, body scales, and upper and lower jaw on the clay snake and skeleton. And have them draw and label the tongue (see diagram).

SNAKES, INSIDE AND OUT

Senses: Tell the kids to think about how they sense the world around them. Then ask them if they think snakes can hear, see, feel, taste, or smell. Tell them that snakes have all of these senses, although some are better developed than others. For example, snakes have fairly good close-up vision, but can't see objects that are far away. And snakes can "hear" vibrations and very low-frequency sound waves through their tiny inner ear bones at the back of their jaws, but they don't have outer ear openings and can't hear most sound waves traveling through the air. Snakes also have a good sense of smell and a limited sense of taste. They use their tongue to do most of the "sniffing," but also pick up scents through their nostrils. (See "How Herps Smell" on page 4 for more about how the tongue picks up scents.)

Teeth and Fangs: Have the kids look at the cobra's teeth and describe some of the ways its teeth are different from their own. (smaller, curved, pointed) Explain that all snakes have teeth. But their teeth are sharp and many point back toward the throat. Tell them snakes use their teeth to kill their prey and/or hold it as they swallow. Point out the fangs in the picture (the two large teeth on the upper jaw). Explain that poisonous snakes have fangs that inject venom into their prey. (Fangs are special kinds of teeth. See "Meat-

Eating Strategies" on page 38 for more about fangs.)

Venom: The venom of different snakes contains different kinds of toxins. Some destroy blood cells, others attack the nervous system, and some do both.

Feeding: Have the kids open their mouths as far as they can and then ask them if they think they could swallow a cantaloupe whole. Tell them if they had jaws like a snake, they could easily swallow something that big. Explain that snakes always swallow their food whole and they often eat things bigger than their heads. They can do this because their jawbones are loosely attached to the skull and to each other. (See "Gulping Their Grub" on page 38 for more about how snakes eat.)

Also explain that all snakes are meat eaters. Some snakes kill their prey by constriction and some by injecting venom. Other snakes just eat their prey alive.

Ribs and Vertebrae: Have the kids point to the cobra's backbone. Ask them to describe it. (It's a series of interlocking bones.) Tell the kids that each bony segment of the backbone is called a *vertebra* (plural is *vertebrae*). Then ask the kids how many ribs are attached to each vertebra. (2) Now ask the kids if they know how many vertebrae and pairs of ribs people have. (Adults have 25 or 26

vertebrae and 12 pairs of ribs.) See if someone can explain what the function of the snake's vertebrae and ribs might be. Explain that a snake's vertebrae and ribs help support its long body and protect its insides from damage. Also explain that muscles attached to the ribs help a snake move. (See "Moving Like a Snake" on page 37 for more about how snakes move.)

Scaly Skin: Snakes are known for their scaly skin. Like most animals' skin, snake skin has several layers. The outer layer of skin is a thin one that the snake sheds as it grows. (How often a snake sheds its skin depends on climate, nutrition, the snake's age, and other factors.) The actual scales are thickened areas of skin below this outer layer. In most snakes the scales are smooth and dry and overlap to help protect the body. The belly scales are often larger and flatter than the other body scales and help snakes move. Each eye is also covered by a hard, round, clear scale.

Innards: Like other slender animals, snakes have organs that have evolved in unusual ways to fit their long, narrow shape. In most snakes, for example, the left lung is very small or gone altogether, and the right lung extends nearly half of the way down the body. The stomach is also long and thin, squeezed in among the other organs.

press sunflower seeds into clay

backbone

THE KING COBRA

- lives in forests in India and Southeast Asia
- can grow to a length of 18 feet (5.4 m)—longer than a pick-up truck
- can have a head the size of a man's hand
- has small fangs in the front of its mouth
- can inject a deadly nerve poison into its victims
- can inject enough venom in one bite to kill a person in about 20 minutes
- feeds on other snakes
- can spread out the ribs in its neck to flatten the skin and form a hood
- can be yellow, brown, olive, dark gray, or black
- builds a nest out of leaves, grass, and soil and then coils around the top until the eggs hatch
- is worshiped by some cultures in Asia

Project Reptile

Solve a reptile graphing puzzle.

Objectives:
Interpret data from a chart. Describe and compare several unusual reptiles.

Ages:
Intermediate and Advanced

Materials:
- *copies of pages 50 and 51*
- *pencils*

Subjects:
Science and Math

D id you know that some adult lizards are so small they can sit on a quarter? Or that some turtles can live for more than a hundred years? Have your group learn about these and other amazing reptiles by solving a puzzle.

Begin the activity by reading "Scaly All-Stars" (below) to your group. After you finish, tell the kids that they can solve a puzzle to discover the identity of the story's mystery reptile.

Next pass out copies of page 50. Explain to the kids that the chart on the Copycat Page organizes some of the information Giovanna found out about reptiles. (*Note:* The entries for age and speed are based on world records. All other entries are based on documented ranges. [Some figures may vary from one source to another.] And all numbers have been rounded off.)

Now pass out copies of page 51. Have your group follow the directions below to solve the puzzle. After the kids have finished, you can go over their answers. (See the margin for answers.)

How To Solve The Puzzle

The list on the left side of the Copycat Page includes some reptile "championship titles," and the "all-star" list on the right includes the reptiles that hold those titles. Use the information in the chart to match each all-star with its title, filling in the blanks in the left-hand column with the appropriate lower-case letter from the right-hand column. As you match each name with a title, you will form a graph coordinate. (For example, the largest lizard [H] is the Komodo dragon [e]. So you should write "e" in the first blank, forming the coordinates [H,e] for point #1.)

After making all the matches, start with #1 and plot that point on the graph at the bottom of the page. (Find "H" on the horizontal axis and mark the point where it intersects "e" on the vertical axis.) Then plot point #2 and draw a line to connect the two points. Next plot point #3 and draw a line from #2 to #3. Continue marking and connecting the points *in order* until you've marked point #16, completing the outline of Giovanna's all-time favorite animal. Finally unscramble the bold letters in the "all-star" list to spell the reptile's name.

Answers

1. (H,e)—Komodo dragon
2. (J,f)—black mamba
3. (K,e)—Aldabra giant tortoise
4. (J,b)—king cobra
5. (I,b)—Kemp's ridley sea turtle
6. (F,a)—Marion's tortoise
7. (C,b)—spotted dwarf adder
8. (A,e)—leatherback
9. (A,g)—blind snake
10. (B,h)—speckled cape tortoise
11. (C,h)—sea snake
12. (D,g)—saltwater crocodile
13. (D,f)—green sea turtle
14. (C,e)—six-lined racerunner
15. (B,f)—least gecko
16. (B,g)—anaconda

Giovanna's favorite animal is a *chameleon.*

Scaly All-Stars

Giovanna, who had always been crazy about snakes and lizards, was a summer volunteer at the zoo near her home. Dr. Hanson, the zoo's reptile-keeper, asked Giovanna if she could think of a way to help people find out just how neat reptiles really are. Giovanna thought a display of reptile "all-stars" would be a super way to teach people about some of these incredible creatures. *I'll call it Project Reptile!* she decided.

Every chance she got, Giovanna worked on Project Reptile. She read and researched until she had a collection of amazing reptile facts and feats. Her favorite animal was part of the reptile all-star team too! The reason she liked the animal was because of its "quick-on-the-draw" sticky tongue. She learned that its tongue can shoot out, zap an insect, and reel in the catch in just one-tenth of a second!

Can you sort through Giovanna's information to complete the list of scaly all-stars and solve the puzzle?

Living Like a Reptile

Make group presentations about snakes, lizards, turtles, and crocodilians.

Objective:
Describe, demonstrate, and compare several reptile adaptations.

Ages:
Advanced

Materials:
- *copy of the investigations on page 46*
- *chalkboard or easel paper*
- *paper and pencils*
- *reference books*
- *clay, cardboard, markers, and other art supplies*

Subject:
Science

Reptiles have some amazing adaptations for staying alive, from sticky toe pads to sticky-tipped tongues. In this activity, your group can investigate some of these adaptations and learn more about what it's like to live like a reptile.

Before you get started, copy the four sets of investigations on page 46 and cut them apart. Using the background information on pages 36-39, review the main characteristics and types of reptiles. Then have the kids think of some things they'd like to find out about these creatures, such as how they move, eat, defend themselves, and reproduce. List their questions on a chalkboard or sheet of easel paper to use later.

Next divide the group into four teams. Explain that each team will research one of these reptile groups: snakes, lizards, turtles, or crocodilians. Then they'll teach what they've discovered to the rest of the group.

Begin by passing out the investigations you copied earlier, giving one set to each team. Explain that the teams are responsible for their own research, using the suggested investigations as a guide. They should also try to keep in mind the questions you listed earlier and try to answer those that pertain to their specific reptile group.

Tell the teams that when they finish their research, they'll need to prepare a presentation for the rest of the group to explain what they discovered. (The members of each team can decide how to divide up the work, but everyone should participate.) During the presentations, the team members can discuss, display, or act out the information they gathered. Provide clay, cardboard, markers, and other supplies and encourage the kids to use models, drawings, demonstrations, and other visual aids to liven up their presentations. For example, the group working on snakes could make the snake craft on page 66 and use it to demonstrate some of the styles of snake locomotion. Or the crocodilian team might want to make a diorama to show how an alligator is adapted to living in a swampy habitat. Remind the kids to concentrate on how the animals in their group live and how they're adapted to their habitats. Also encourage them to use examples of specific reptiles in their explanations.

Finally provide the teams with reference books on reptiles (see the bibliography on page 67 for suggestions), paper, and pencils, and give the kids several days to research and plan their presentations.

(continued next page)

Russell's viper

REPTILIAN INVESTIGATIONS

Snakes
- Demonstrate some of the different ways snakes move on land.
- Describe two methods snakes use to kill their prey.
- Demonstrate how a snake can swallow something larger than its head.
- Compare three ways snakes defend themselves.

Lizards
- Demonstrate how a gecko can cling to a vertical or upside-down surface.
- Compare how two kinds of lizards use their tongues.
- Compare three ways lizards defend themselves.
- Demonstrate how a male lizard attracts a mate or defends its territory.

Turtles
- Demonstrate how a turtle's shell protects its body.
- Compare the adaptations of a turtle that lives on land with those of a turtle that spends its life in the ocean.
- Compare the diets of three kinds of turtles.
- Describe how a sea turtle builds its nest and lays its eggs.

Crocodilians
- Demonstrate how a crocodile finds food.
- Compare the habits of an alligator, crocodile, and gavial, and describe how to tell the three animals apart.
- Compare an alligator's nest with the nest of a crocodile.
- Describe how alligators defend their young.

BRANCHING OUT: MAKE A GUIDE TO REPTILES

You might want to have the kids develop a group "field guide" to local reptiles. Contact a nature center, museum, or university biology department to find out which species live in your area. Have each child choose one species and find out these things about the animal:

Description: What does the reptile look like?

Range and Habitat: Where does the reptile live and what kind of habitat does it prefer?

Locomotion: How does the reptile get around?

Feeding: What does the reptile eat and how does it find or capture its food?

Defense: What animals prey on the reptile and how does it defend itself?

Social and Reproductive Behavior: How does the reptile interact with others of its kind? (Describe how it finds and courts a mate, how it defends its territory, and if it gives birth or lays eggs and cares for its young.)

Facts and Feats: Describe any distinctive adaptations or behaviors of the reptile.

After the kids have researched their reptiles, have them write the information in a field guide format, with short descriptions for each category listed. Then have them draw a picture of their animal to go with the written description and have them label key features to identify various adaptations (see example). Combine their completed field guide entries to make a super display of resident reptiles.

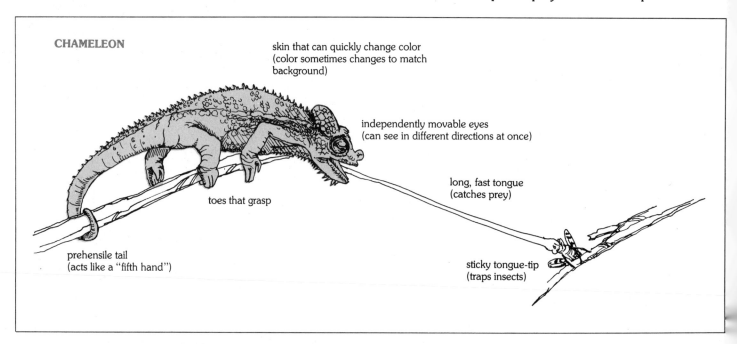

CHAMELEON

skin that can quickly change color (color sometimes changes to match background)

independently movable eyes (can see in different directions at once)

long, fast tongue (catches prey)

toes that grasp

prehensile tail (acts like a "fifth hand")

sticky tongue-tip (traps insects)

box turtle

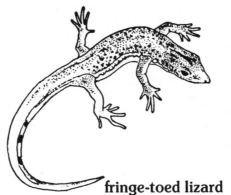

fringe-toed lizard

gavial

gecko

rattlesnake

green anole

alligator

blue-tongued skink

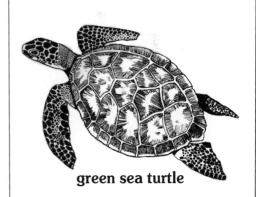

green sea turtle

snapping turtle

anaconda

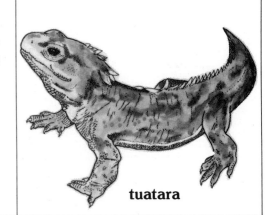

tuatara

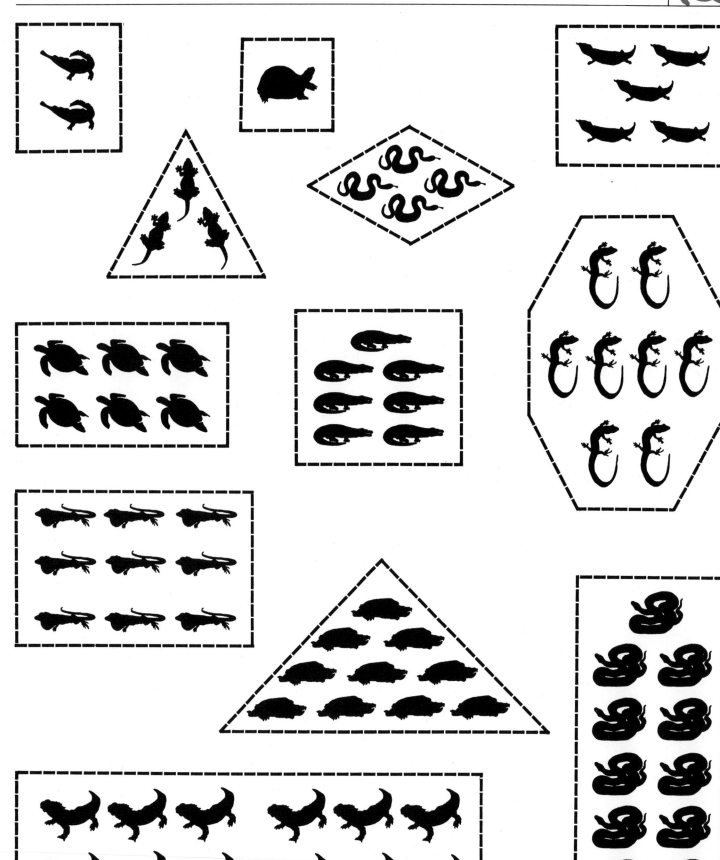

RANGER RICK'S NATURESCOPE: LET'S HEAR IT FOR HERPS!
(See Reptile Countdown—p 40)

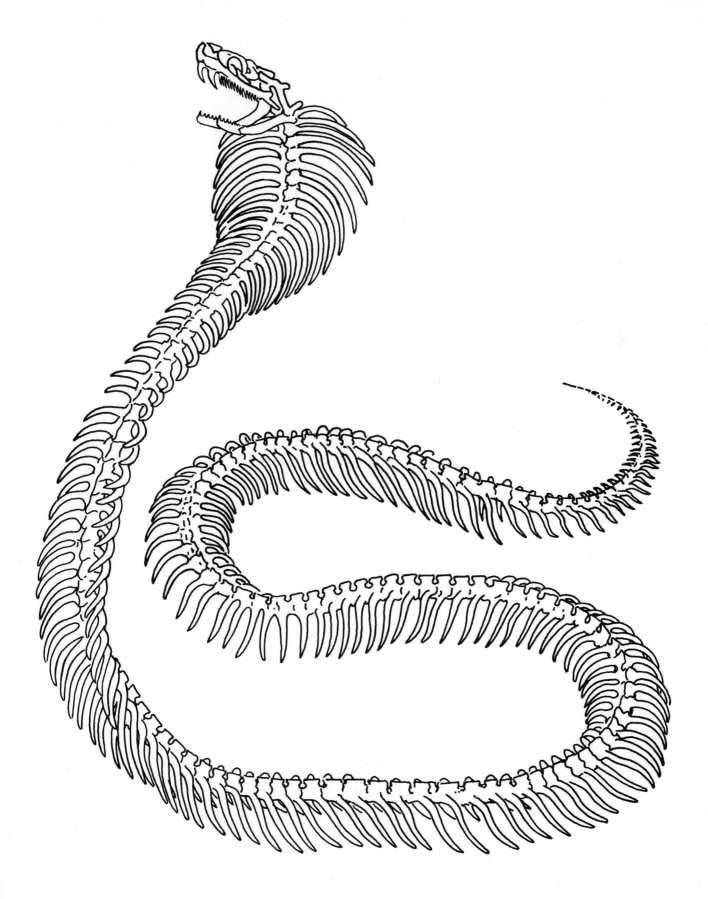

(See Close-Up on Cobras—p 42)

COPYCAT PAGE

PROJECT REPTILE—SHEET 1

	TURTLES	SNAKES	LIZARDS	CROCODILIANS
SIZE (smallest to largest)	**land** speckled cape tortoise (4 inches) Aldabra giant tortoise (55 inches) **fresh water** flattened musk turtle (4 inches) alligator snapping turtle (26 inches) **ocean** Kemp's ridley sea turtle (29 inches) leatherback sea turtle (96 inches, 1800 pounds)	**poisonous** spotted dwarf adder (10 inches) king cobra (18 feet) **non-poisonous** blind snake (5 inches) anaconda (38 feet, 350 pounds)	least gecko (½ inch) Komodo dragon (10 feet, 360 pounds)	dwarf caiman (6½ feet) saltwater crocodile (25 feet, 3000 pounds)
AGE (oldest on record)	Marion's tortoise (in captivity since 1766; died 1918)	boa constrictor (born 1936; died 1977)	slow worm (in captivity since 1892; died 1946)	American alligator (born 1912; died 1978)
VENOM (most poisonous)	There are no poisonous turtles.	The bites of vipers, cobras, and some sea snakes can sometimes kill people. Some scientists think that the venom of one kind of sea snake is much stronger than that of other snakes.	Only two lizards are poisonous (Gila monster and Mexican beaded lizard). Their bite is usually not dangerous to people.	There are no poisonous crocodilians.
SPEED (fastest on record)	green sea turtle (22 mph, swimming)	black mamba (7 mph, crawling)	six-lined racerunner (18 mph, running)	Johnson's crocodile (11 mph, running)

TITLES

1. largest lizard: H,____
2. fastest snake: J,____
3. largest land turtle: K,____
4. longest poisonous snake: J,____
5. smallest sea turtle: I,____
6. longest-lived reptile: F,____
7. smallest poisonous snake: C,____
8. largest sea turtle: A,____
9. smallest snake: A,____
10. smallest land turtle: B,____
11. most poisonous reptile: C,____
12. heaviest reptile: D,____
13. fastest reptile: D,____
14. fastest reptile on land: C,____
15. smallest reptile: B,____
16. longest reptile: B,____

ALL-STARS

(b) king **c**obra
(f) green sea turtle
(g) **an**aconda
(e) six-**l**ined racerunner
(a) Marion's tortois**e**
(g) saltwater crocodile
(e) leat**h**erback sea turtle
(h) speckled cape tortoise
(f) least geck**o**
(e) Komodo dragon
(b) Kemp's ridley sea turtl**e**
(h) sea snake
(f) black **m**amba
(g) blind snake
(e) Aldabra giant tortoise
(b) spotted dwarf **a**dder

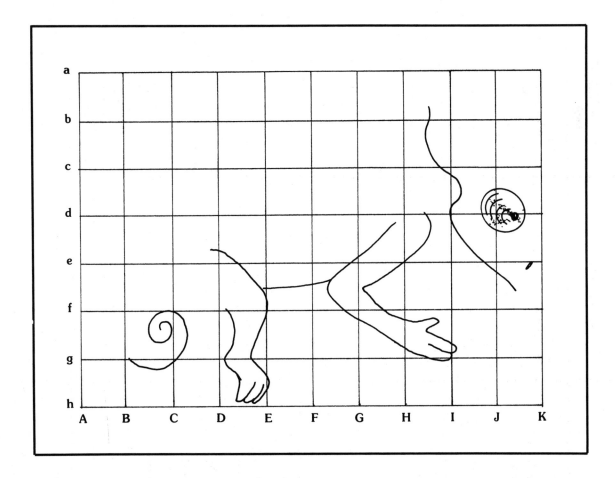

WHAT IS IT?   __ __ __ __ __ __ __ __ __ __ __

HERPS IN OUR LIVES

I f you're up on gourmet trends, then you already know that herps are "in." Turtle soup, frog's legs, terrapin stew, rattlesnake steaks, alligator sauce picante, and other popular herp entrees have become standard fare in many restaurants and gourmet shops around the world. But eating herps is not a new idea. In many countries, people have been eating lizards, snakes, and other herps for centuries. But in the last few years, the market for herp meat has been growing by leaps and bounds. To satisfy the increased demand, thousands of sea turtles, snapping turtles, frogs, and other herps are captured and sold every year.

HERPS IN TROUBLE

The growing market for herp meat is just one of the reasons for the increase in herp trafficking—the buying and selling of herp products and live specimens. In addition to eating herps, people also make fancy shoes, purses, and luggage from herp hides and carve jewelry from turtle shells. And many people buy live lizards, snakes, crocodiles, and turtles to keep as pets or exhibit at roadside zoos. Collectors also make money selling herps to novelty shops and to supply companies that provide schools and other educational institutions with frogs, snakes, and other herp specimens. And although much of this trade is regulated, some is not.

Overharvesting by itself is a serious enough strain on herp populations. But when coupled with increasing habitat loss around the world, the problem becomes even more severe. (Habitat loss is *the* most serious threat facing amphibians and reptiles.) Many reptiles and amphibians are already threatened with extinction. For example, people have killed more than 20 million alligators, crocodiles, and gavials in the last 50 years for their hides. In addition, thousands of acres of wetland and river habitat where these animals live have been drained, filled, or polluted. As a result, American crocodiles, gavials, and some species of South American caimans are very close to extinction. And many other herps are also in trouble, including sea turtles in oceans all over the world, some of the monitor lizards in Southeast Asia, giant tortoises of the Galapagos Islands, and eastern indigo snakes, gopher tortoises, Houston toads, and several freshwater turtles in the United States.

One reason there's not more public concern over herps is that many people find toads, frogs, snakes, and other herps unappealing. In fact, many people go out of their way to kill snakes and other herps because of fear and dislike.

In a way, it's not surprising that herps have such a bad public image, considering the number of myths that have circulated over the years. For example, toads are rumored to cause warts and to help witches with their evil spells, cobras are supposed to avenge the death of their "relatives," and snakes and lizards in general are often characterized as slimy, vindictive, or just plain evil, sometimes stinging enemies with their forked tongues and pointed tails. And as if this herp gossip weren't bad enough, writers often created imaginary herps that could do terrible things, like the monstrous *Crocodylus* that could swallow people alive and *Draco the Dragon,* a serpentlike reptile that was strong enough to suffocate an elephant.

HERPS, PAST AND PRESENT

Despite all the bad press, there have been some bright spots in herp history. For example, some cultures in the past worshiped and respected herps. The image of the sacred asp appears in many ancient Egyptian works of art and architecture. And in Roman and Greek cultures, snakes, turtles, and frogs were often thought to have great healing powers. Turtles and snakes were also revered by ancient Chinese and Hindu civilizations, which believed they were sacred. And many herps were an integral part of religious and cultural traditions in North and South American Indian tribes. (For more about herps in history, see "People and Herps" on page 54.)

Another bright spot is that more and more people today are recognizing the value of protecting herps and are helping to prevent habitat loss and over-collecting. (For more about habitat loss and endangered species, see *Nature-Scope: Endangered Species—Wild and Rare* [Vol. 3, No. 3].) For example, instead of dissecting frogs in biology classes, some schools are opting to use computer programs or stuffed fabric models. And some restaurants are refusing to serve dishes made from herps and other wildlife. The U.S. Fish and Wildlife Service, the National Wildlife Federation, organizations in other countries, herpetology societies around the world, and many other groups and private citizens are also working hard to protect endangered and threatened species. For instance, special habitat reserves have been set aside for some herps, such as the desert tortoise, Indian gavial, and Komodo dragon. For other species, such as the American alligator, strict enforcement of trade laws has helped stop illegal trafficking. In some areas, people are trying new and often controversial techniques, such as experimental herp farming—raising crocodiles, turtles, and lizards in controlled environments. (Although these farms seem to have potential for helping protect wild populations, many people are concerned that they are indirectly harming wild herps. That's because some collectors are trying to pass off illegally collected wild herps as those that have been raised on farms.)

Even though there's still a lot of work to do, we're finally figuring out what the Romans, Greeks, and Egyptians knew all along—that herps are amazing and important in a lot of different ways, and that there's a lot more to herps than creepy myths and good eats.

Indian cobra

People and Herps

Objectives:
Discuss some of the misconceptions people have about herps. Describe some of the ways people have viewed herps through history.

Ages:
Primary and Intermediate

Materials:
- *chalkboard or easel paper*
- *crayons or markers*
- *construction paper*
- *stapler*
- *tape or glue*
- *paper and pencils (optional)*
- *paper plates (optional)*
- *long pencils, sticks, or rulers (optional)*
- *masking tape (optional)*

Subjects:
Science and History

People have always had a love/hate relationship with herps. Throughout history, we've worshiped them, condemned them, studied them, and feared them. Try this survey with your kids to help them explore their own feelings about herps and to make them aware of some common misconceptions about these animals. Afterward the kids can put together a booklet that focuses on some historical aspects of people's relationships with herps.

PART 1: A SHORT SURVEY

Write each of the sentences listed under "What Do You Think?" (on the next page) onto a chalkboard or sheet of easel paper. You can have the kids respond to the questions in one of two ways. Younger kids, for example, might have fun making paper plate signs that, when held up, reflect whether they think the answer to a sentence is true or false. (See "How to Make a Survey Sign," on page 56.) You can tally their answers as you read each sentence, writing the number of "trues" (happy-face signs) and "falses" (unhappy-face signs) under each one.

Older kids can number a page from one to eleven and write "true" or "false" beside the appropriate number. After they finish, tally the answers and talk about each one. (Explanations are in parentheses after each sentence.) Then let the kids get started on the next part of the activity.

PART 2: HERPS THROUGH HISTORY

Have the kids follow these directions to make a herp history booklet:
1. Draw a picture of some (or all) of the facts listed on the right and on the top of page 55.
2. Fold several pieces of colored construction paper in half widthwise and staple them together.
3. Tape or glue each picture onto one of the construction paper pages.
4. Label each "herps through history" picture and print a title for your booklet on the cover.

- According to Hindu legend, the world rests on the back of four elephants that are standing on the back of a giant turtle.
- Hannibal, a ruler in North Africa more than 2000 years ago, thought of a way to beat the Romans in a battle. His idea was to fill pots with snakes and throw them onto enemy ships. The idea worked! When the pots smashed and the snakes crawled out, the Romans went into a panic and surrendered.
- People once thought that salamanders could crawl through fires without being burned. Some people also thought that salamanders could put the fires out as they crawled through them.
- Legend claims that, long ago, Saint

Patrick drove all of the snakes out of Ireland.

- In parts of Europe, people once buried dead lizards under their houses to scare witches away.
- Many people who lived in ancient Rome used frogs to try to cure toothaches. They'd do this by spitting in a frog's mouth and asking it to take the toothache away.
- In 1775, the rattlesnake was proposed as a symbol of America's 13 colonies. People who supported this idea thought the rattlesnake would be a good symbol for several reasons. For example, the snake's segmented tail was thought to be like the colonies:

Each part is independent of the others, but all are part of the whole.

- In the Middle Ages, some people thought toads had a magic jewel in their head. If you wore a ring made from one of these jewels, you'd be protected from poison.
- Some of the Indians that lived along North America's West Coast worshiped a spirit they called Frog Woman. According to their legends, Frog Woman created Earth.
- Cleopatra, a queen of ancient Egypt, killed herself by allowing a poisonous snake to bite her.
- Burmese legend says that a frog causes eclipses by swallowing the moon.

(continued next page)

WHAT DO YOU THINK?

1. *Reptiles and amphibians are scary and creepy.* (There's no right or wrong response to this one. Many people *do* think that snakes, frogs, lizards, and other herps are ugly, frightening, weird, and so on. But explain to the kids that, in general, negative feelings about herps—or about any other animals, for that matter—tend to subside as people learn more about the animals and the fascinating ways they're adapted to surviving.)

2. *All turtles are slow.* (False. Many turtles *are* slow. Some of the big tortoises, for example, walk at a pace of only about one-eighth of a mile [.2 km] an hour. People, on the other hand, can stroll along at about three miles [5 km] an hour. But a few turtles can really move. For example, green sea turtles can swim through the sea at nearly 20 miles [32 km] per hour.)

3. *Lizards and snakes are slimy.* (False. Like all reptiles, snakes and lizards have dry skin. But many amphibians—salamanders and some frogs, for example—*are* slimy. Their skin contains glands that produce mucus, which helps to keep the animals from drying out.)

4. *Most snakes are poisonous to people.* (False. Less than 10% of all snakes have venom that's capable of harming people.)

5. *Some turtles can live for more than 100 years.* (True. Box turtles can live to be more than a century old, and so can some other kinds of turtles. The oldest-known turtle was thought to be at least 152 years old when it died. This ancient animal, a captive Marion's tortoise, might have lived a lot longer if it hadn't accidentally taken a fatal fall.)

6. *Some frogs produce a more powerful poison than some snakes.* (True. A few frogs produce very potent poisons from special skin glands. In some cases these poisons are more potent than those of the most poisonous snakes. Native peoples often coat their darts with the powerful poisons of certain frogs.)

7. *Farmers should get rid of all snakes from their barns.* (Just as with the first sentence, there's no right or wrong answer to this one. But it provides a good opportunity to talk about how snakes and people can "work together." Point out to your kids that many farmers are glad when certain kinds of non-poisonous snakes take up residence on their farms. The snakes eat rats and mice, which can gobble up a lot of the grain that the farmers have stored away. Certain snakes may eat some chicken eggs and young, but the benefits of having non-poisonous snakes around the barnyard often outweigh the disadvantages.)

8. *If you handle a toad, you'll get warts.* (False. This misconception has persisted for a long time, but it's not true. A toad's "warty" skin isn't contagious.)

9. *Only a few reptiles and amphibians are endangered or threatened.* (False. The U.S. Fish and Wildlife Service's *List of Endangered and Threatened Wildlife and Plants* lists more than 100 species of reptiles and amphibians as endangered or threatened. And several herp species are currently being reviewed for possible listing in the future.)

10. *Most kinds of reptiles and amphibians become endangered because people kill them for food and other products.* (False. Many herps *are* killed for food and other products such as leather. But habitat loss is the most serious problem herps—and almost all other wild animals and plants—face today. [For more about why many herps are in trouble, see "Herps in Trouble" on page 52.])

11. *It's easy to tell a poisonous snake from a non-poisonous snake.* (False. Some poisonous snakes have several distinctive features that make them easier to recognize than other poisonous snakes. For example, pit vipers in North America have flat, triangular heads, thick bodies, vertical eye-pupils, and a series of single belly scales from head to tail. But many other poisonous snakes don't fit this description. And there are also some non-poisonous snakes that have heads and bodies that look like those of some poisonous snakes. The best way to know whether a snake is poisonous or not is to learn to recognize the poisonous snakes that live in your area.)

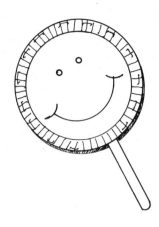

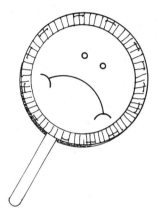

1. Draw a happy face on the back of one paper plate and a sad face on the back of another plate.

2. Tape a pencil, stick, or ruler to the inside of one of the plates (i.e., the side you would eat from). Masking tape works best.
3. Put the two plates together with the faces on the outside, and staple around the edges. (Make sure both faces are right side up.)
4. When you read the sentences, the kids should hold up the "happy side" of their paper plates to the front of the room if they think the sentence is true and the "sad side" if they think it's false.

Hooray for Herps!

Organize a public relations campaign to help give reptiles and amphibians a more positive image.

Objectives:
Discuss why some people dislike herps. Name several positive things about reptiles and amphibians.

Ages:
Intermediate and Advanced

Materials:
- *reference books*
- *poster paper (optional)*
- *markers or paints (optional)*

Subjects:
Science and Language Arts

How often do you hear someone say something good about a snake? Or a toad, lizard, frog, or crocodile, for that matter? Probably not too often. Over the years, some herps have been given a pretty bad reputation.

In this activity your kids can do something to improve people's opinions about herps by organizing a herp public relations campaign. Begin by discussing the kids' reactions to different kinds of herps. How do they feel about frogs, snakes, salamanders, toads, and alligators? You'll probably find that the kids, like many other people, have a lot of negative feelings about certain herps, such as snakes and toads. (You may want to refer to "People and Herps" on page 54 for more questions on how people feel about herps and for misconceptions about reptiles and amphibians.)

Then explain that many people have negative reactions to herps because they just don't know much about these creatures. Tell the kids that their challenge is to help change the way people think about herps by launching a public relations campaign for reptiles and amphibians. Divide the kids into groups of four or five and assign each group one of the herps listed on the next page.

Tell the groups that they should first try to find out how people feel about their reptile or amphibian. To do this, they should look for ways their herp is portrayed in cartoons, movies, TV shows, advertisements, and newspapers. They could even survey their friends and family

alligator
American toad
boa constrictor
crocodile
gecko
Gila monster
hellbender
mudpuppy
newt
python
rat snake
rattlesnake
skink
snapping turtle
water moccasin

to find out how they feel about their animal. And they could "dig up" any myths or folklore that could explain how people feel about their herp. For example, many people believe that touching a toad will give you warts.

Then have the kids find some facts about their herp—what it eats, where it lives, and any other important facts. Finally, have the kids in each team use the information they've discovered to develop a PR campaign to give their herp a better image. They can design posters, make

up TV or radio commercials, sing songs, or create fliers—anything to play up the positive features of their herp and expose the myths. For example, the rattlesnake group could make posters showing the number of rodents an average snake eats in its lifetime. And the crocodile team could put on a skit that illustrates some neat facts about crocodiles and that plays down their "ferocious" image.

Give the kids time to put their information together. Then have the groups present their campaigns on "Herp Day."

Race to the Sea

Play a board game that focuses on some of the dangers baby sea turtles face.

Objective:
Discuss some of the dangers that threaten sea turtles.

Ages:
Intermediate

Materials:
- *copies of pages 60 and 61*
- *cardboard*
- *dice*
- *crayons or markers*
- *paper*
- *pencils*
- *pictures of sea turtles*
- *pictures of land turtles*
- *scissors*
- *glue*
- *index cards (optional)*
- *copies of the turtle playing pieces on page 58*

Subject:
Science

 ife's tough for baby sea turtles. Female turtles don't stick around to take care of the eggs they lay, and the baby turtles must fend for themselves, right from the start. As soon as they hatch, the young turtles start digging their way out of their sandy beach nests. And from there they head for the ocean—a perilous trek that exposes the soft-shelled babies to hungry birds and other predators, curious people, beach-going vehicles, and many other dangers. By playing "Race to the Sea," your kids can learn about sea turtles and the obstacles hatchlings must overcome on their journey to the ocean.

Before the kids start playing the game, show them pictures of sea turtles and use the information in "Turtle Talk" on page 59 to talk about sea turtles in general. Then pass out copies of pages 60 and 61 and have them color their own game boards. (You might want to have the kids work in pairs to color a single game board.) Remind them to color lightly so they don't obscure the lettering on the board.

Also make copies of the turtle playing pieces shown in the margin on page 58. Pass them out and have the kids color them. (To make the pieces easier to tell apart, tell the kids to make each one a different color.) Then have them cut out the playing pieces and glue them to pieces of cardboard. You might also want to have

them glue their game boards to cardboard to make the boards sturdier.

When everyone is finished, go over the rules for "Race to the Sea" on the next page and let the kids try their luck at the game. Afterward, discuss the obstacles the baby turtles encountered in the game and point out that real turtles face these and other dangers. Some baby turtles do manage to make it to the sea—but then they face a whole new set of hazards! Use the information under "Troubles for Turtles" to discuss some of the problems young and adult sea turtles come up against. Then explain that many people are working to help sea turtles survive. For example, in some places laws have been passed that prohibit people from tampering with either the turtles or their nests. Some areas have passed laws forbidding bright lights and vehicles on beaches where turtles nest. And some conservation groups have sea turtle rescue programs that help hatchlings reach the water. (For information about HEART, a group that's helping the endangered Kemp's ridley sea turtle, see "People Power" on page 53 of *NatureScope: Endangered Species—Wild and Rare* [Vol. 3, No. 3]. And for general information about how people can help endangered and threatened sea turtles, see "Wheel of Trouble" on page 37 of the same issue.)

(continued next page)

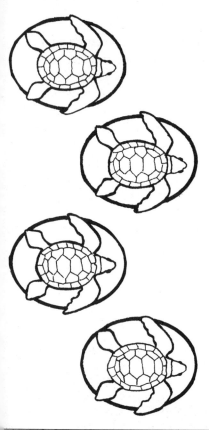

HOW TO PLAY "RACE TO THE SEA"

The "Race to the Sea" game board represents a beach where a sea turtle has laid her eggs, and each turtle playing piece represents 25 hatchlings. The object of the game is to reach the sea with the most turtles. (*Note:* The path taken by the turtles on the game board twists, turns, and curves. Explain to the kids that real baby turtles usually head for the ocean on a fairly straight course. But for the purposes of this game, we've made the turtles' path somewhat indirect.)

The game can have up to four players, and each player should "operate" only one of the turtle playing pieces. Here's how to play:

- Play starts at the "nest," in the lower left-hand corner of the board. Roll a single die to determine who goes first.

- Move your turtle playing piece by rolling a die and moving the turtle that number of spaces. (Move pieces in the direction shown by those spaces illustrated with a turtle.)

- When you come to a "crossroad" for the first time (all crossroads are marked with arrows), move your turtle in the direction of the solid arrow. (Count the arrow as one space.) On the "return" trip through the crossroad, skip the solid arrow space and move over it in the direction of the broken arrow. This time through the crossroad, don't count either the solid or broken arrow as a space.

- Each time you move your turtle to a new space, follow the directions written on that space even if another player's turtle is also on it. Information on some of the spaces tells you to move forward, backward, miss a turn, or lose a certain number of turtles. If you land on a space that says you lose turtles, keep track of the number lost on a piece of paper. And if you miss a turn, you must remain on that space while the other players take their next turns.

- If you lose all 25 of your turtles before reaching the sea, you're out of the game.

- The player who reaches the sea with the most baby turtles is the winner. If there's a tie (two or more players finishing with the same number of turtles), the player who reached the sea first is the winner. You don't need an exact roll to reach the sea.

Add an Extra Challenge!

You can add an extra challenge by having the kids make up question cards to use during the game. First pass out several index cards to each person and have the kids do some general research on sea turtles before they play the game. Then tell the kids to write a question and answer, based on what they found out through their research, on each card. When they play "Race to the Sea," a player who lands on a space with a turtle on it will be required to answer one of the questions. (Make sure the kids don't come

up with questions that are too obscure or difficult. Questions such as "What are two kinds of sea turtles?" and "What is the largest kind of sea turtle?" are OK, but questions such as "How much does the average leatherback sea turtle weigh?" are not.) Tell the kids to write the answers on the same side of the index cards as they write the questions.

When they're finished, mix up the index cards and stack several of them beside the game board. When a player lands on a turtle space, another player can read one of the questions. There's no penalty for a wrong answer, but a correct answer means the player can move ahead two spaces. Whenever this happens, the player should ignore any negative "instructions" that are printed on the space he or she moved to. But a player can act on "positive" instructions, such as "Move ahead one space."

TURTLE TALK

There are seven species of sea turtles in the world's oceans: the loggerhead, green, Kemp's ridley, olive ridley, Australian flatback, hawksbill, and leatherback. And all but the Australian flatback are listed as either threatened or endangered. The following facts apply generally to most of these sea turtles:

- eat jellyfish, sponges, crabs, fish, and/or plants, depending on the species
- length can range from about 2 to 8 feet (.6-2.4 m) and weight can range from about 100 to 1800 pounds (45-810 kg), depending on the species
- some species may live as many as 70 years
- have paddle-shaped flippers that help them move through the water and streamlined shells that reduce water resistance (compare to pictures of land turtles with high-domed shells and clawed feet)

- lay their eggs on sandy beaches; use their back flippers to dig deep holes in the sand where they lay up to 100 eggs
- eggs hatch in about two months
- hatchlings dig their way out of their nest and head immediately for the surf
- many young turtles are eaten by birds, crabs, fish, and other predators
- at best, only two or three hatchlings from any one turtle nest will survive to adulthood
- adult turtles have only two enemies—sharks and people

For more information about how sea turtles lay their eggs, see "Look Out for Loggerheads," *Ranger Rick,* July 1983, pp 4-7.

This information and the information under "Troubles for Turtles" (below) were adapted from the activity entitled "Wheel of Trouble" on page 37 of *NatureScope: Endangered Species—Wild and Rare* (Vol. 3, No. 3).

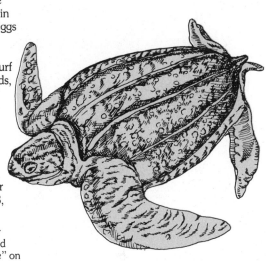
leatherback sea turtle

TROUBLES FOR TURTLES

Here's a rundown of the major problems certain species of sea turtles face during their lives. Some of these problems are more severe for certain species. For example, hawksbill turtles are overhunted for their shells and eggs. But because they live in areas where shrimp fishing is not a big business, they're rarely caught in shrimp nets. For simplicity, we didn't include which problems affect which species.
Turtle Products: Overharvesting is a major threat to sea turtles. They are killed for their beautiful shells (which are made into jewelry), for their skin (which is tanned and used to make boots, belts, shoes, and bags), and for food (people eat their meat and eggs and use the cartilage to make soup).
Changing Beaches: Development is another problem for sea turtles. In many areas, people have built homes, roads, motels, and other types of development on the beaches where sea turtles nest. If a

female turtle lays her eggs on a built-up beach, the hatchlings often have problems. Most turtles hatch at night and instinctively head for the ocean. Many scientists think the hatchlings may be guided by the brightness of the sky over the water. But on developed beaches, the newly hatched turtles are mistakenly guided by the bright lights of buildings and street lights. These hatchlings often dry up in the sun the next day or get eaten by predators.
Hungry Hunters and Others: Predators—gulls, raccoons, dogs, and crabs, for example—eat a lot of turtle eggs and baby turtles. People can be "predators" too: Beachcombers sometimes collect baby sea turtles to dry and sell as stuffed souvenirs.
Beach Buggies: Vehicles on beaches also cause problems for baby turtles. Some nests and hatchlings are crushed under tires. And sometimes hatchlings fall

into deep ruts created by the tires. (Often the tiny turtles, which are usually no more than a couple of inches long, can't crawl out of tire ruts once they fall into them.)
Pollution: When plastic garbage is dumped into the oceans, it can cause big problems for many sea turtles. That's because turtles may mistake floating plastic bags for jellyfish and swallow them. They can't digest the plastic, and if it blocks a turtle's esophagus, the animal will slowly starve.

Other forms of pollution, such as oil, tar, and poisonous chemicals, are also dangerous, especially to young turtles.
Fishing Nets: Every year, some sea turtles drown when they are accidentally caught in shrimp nets. To help solve this problem, some shrimpers are now using Turtle Excluder Devices (TEDs). TEDs fit inside shrimp nets and release the trapped turtles.

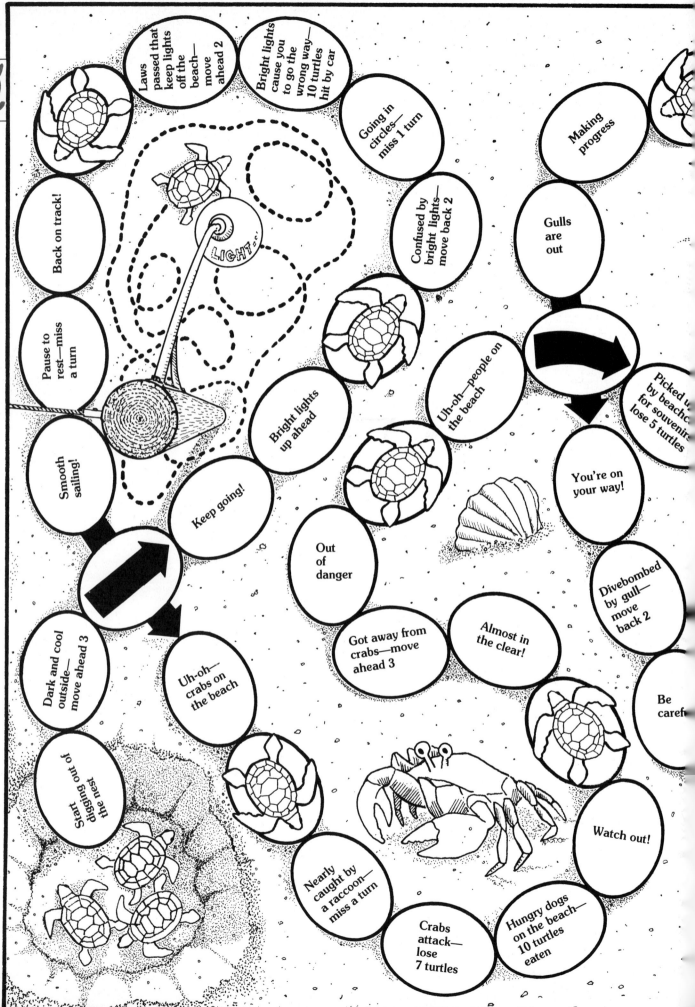

Laws passed that keep lights off the beach—move ahead 2

Bright lights cause you to go the wrong way—10 turtles hit by car

Going in circles—miss 1 turn

Making progress

Back on track!

LIGHT

Gulls are out

Confused by bright lights—move back 2

Pause to rest—miss a turn

Uh-oh—people on the beach

Picked up by beachc_ for souvenir_ lose 5 turtles

Smooth sailing!

Bright lights up ahead

You're on your way!

Keep going!

Out of danger

Divebombed by gull—move back 2

Dark and cool outside—move ahead 3

Uh-oh—crabs on the beach

Got away from crabs—move ahead 3

Almost in the clear!

Be caref_

Start out of digging the nest

Watch out!

Nearly caught by a raccoon—miss a turn

Crabs attack—lose 7 turtles

Hungry dogs on the beach—10 turtles eaten

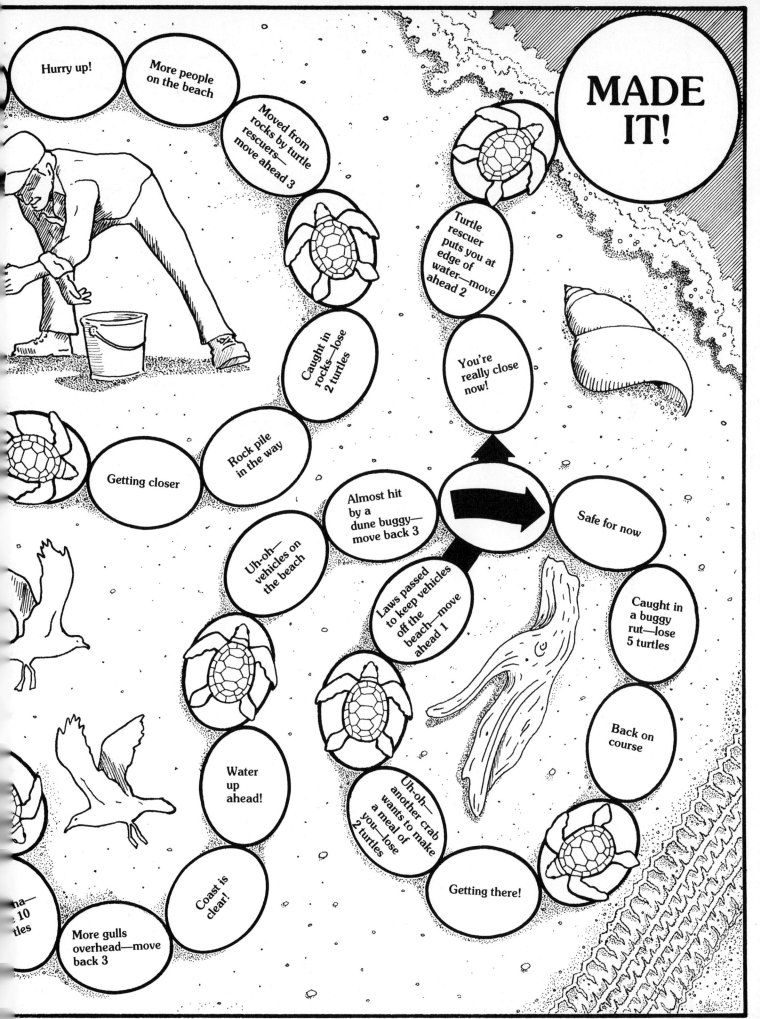

What Would You Do?

Read and discuss several hypothetical situations involving reptiles and amphibians.

Objectives:

Discuss some of the problems reptiles and amphibians face. Give examples of how personal feelings and beliefs can affect situations involving herps.

Ages:

Intermediate and Advanced

Materials:

- *copies of the herp scenarios on pages 63 and 64*
- *chalkboard or easel paper (optional)*

Subjects:

Language Arts and Social Studies

In this discussion activity, your group can explore how they feel about a variety of issues involving reptiles and amphibians. Before starting, make copies of the scenarios on pages 63 and 64. Also make sure that everyone is familiar with the characteristics of reptiles and amphibians and with the different types of herps that make up each group. (You might want to do several activities from other chapters as an introduction.)

Begin the activity by passing out copies of the scenarios to each person. Explain that they will be reading about a variety of situations that deal with reptiles and amphibians, and that they will have to decide what they would do if faced with the situation described. Emphasize that there are no "right" or "wrong" answers in this activity. The purpose is to learn about certain issues involving herps, to explore how they feel about these issues, and to discuss their feelings and opinions with others to get different perspectives.

Have each person read the scenarios and decide how he or she would deal with each situation, picking the option or op-

tions that most closely match how he or she would react. If none of the options apply, tell the kids to think about other actions they would take.

After the kids have had time to think about each situation, have them share their reactions. (You might want to keep a tally on a chalkboard or large piece of easel paper.) Encourage discussion and provide time for each person to discuss why he or she responded in a certain way. Ask the kids what kinds of things they kept in mind as they made their decisions. For example, did they choose what they thought were the most responsible actions to take? Did they think about laws that might affect the situation? Did they need more information before they felt comfortable making a decision? Afterward, ask if the group discussion helped provide new perspectives or if, after listening to other people's opinions, any of the group members had changed their mind about what they might do.

As you discuss the scenarios, you might want to bring up some of the following points:

Herp Pets

- Herp pets need a lot of care. For example, they need clean water, clean cages, the right temperature and amount of humidity, and a balanced diet. Many won't eat in captivity and some require hard-to-get food. Herps also get a variety of diseases in captivity.
- Many herps, such as turtles, carry diseases that can be transmitted to people. Some herps can also bite, and some are poisonous.
- It is very difficult to raise most reptiles from eggs, unless you have special equipment to control temperature and humidity.
- Many scientists do not recommend touching herp eggs because it can harm the developing embryos. For example, just handling some amphibian eggs can kill them because the protective jelly gets damaged.
- Buying non-native pets or collecting them in the wild and bringing

them home with you can create a variety of problems. For one thing, it's often hard to supply them with the foods they normally eat. And it's also a problem if they escape into the wild. Introduced species have no natural predators, and if released, they can compete with—and often harm—native species.
- Many herp pets are very expensive.
- Many herp pets are sold illegally. And many herps that are collected illegally for the pet trade die before they are even sold.

Herp Laws

- It is illegal to collect animals from national parks and wildlife refuges, as well as from most state and local parks.
- Federally listed threatened and endangered reptiles and amphibians are protected by the Endangered Species Act. It's against the law to buy, sell, possess, or abuse them in any way. There are also international trading laws that protect rare, threatened, and endangered

species. (See *NatureScope: Endangered Species—Wild and Rare* [Vol. 3, No. 3] for more information.)
- It is sometimes impossible to tell if a product is made from an endangered or threatened species. For example, people who sell illegal wildlife products will often tell you their products are from captive-bred species. Conservationists say the best bet is not to buy anything you think could have come from a protected animal.

Other Herp Tips

- If you see a poisonous snake, herpetologists recommend that you back away quietly and don't try to confront it. Many people are bitten when they try to kill a snake.
- Most snakes are not poisonous. (Less than 10% of all snakes have venom that's capable of harming people.)
- Snakes are very important rodent-controllers. Many feed on rats, mice, and other pests.

ANOTHER OPTION

Depending on the make-up of your group, you might want to try this activity using small discussion groups. Have one person in each group read a scenario to the other group members and tally how each person in the group would react to the scenario. Encourage the groups to discuss their answers.

After about five minutes, have the groups move on to another scenario, and have another person in each group act as the reader and tally person. After all the groups have finished discussing each scenario, talk about each one with the entire group.

HERP SCENARIOS: WHAT WOULD YOU DO?

1. **Your best friend is about to go on vacation to a park in Texas. She's been reading about lizards of the West and tells you she's going to try to catch a horned "toad" while she's there. She tells you all about the habits of these lizards, such as what they eat, where they live, and how they defend themselves. She also explains how she's going to take care of it when she gets it home, showing you the book she checked out from the library on how to care for lizards.**
What Would You Do?
   - encourage her to bring the lizard back so you can learn more about it too
   - tell her that you don't think it's right to take an animal out of the wild to keep as a pet
   - read more about the lizard so you can help her take care of it
   - ask her to bring you one, if she finds two
   - tell her it's illegal to collect any living thing in a park, but let her make up her own mind
   - other

2. **Bali and his sister find some leathery, white eggs buried in the leaves under a log. Bali thinks they might be snake eggs, but he's not sure. He's always wanted to have a pet snake, but the only pet he's ever had was a turtle.**
What Should Bali Do?
   - collect the eggs and put them in a terrarium when he gets home
   - leave the eggs where they are, but mark the spot so he can return to check on them often
   - collect one of the eggs and take it home to try to hatch it
   - collect the eggs and take them to the nature center near his house
   - other

3. **You are on a hike with your friends and older sister when your sister spots a timber rattlesnake. The snake is close to the trail, sunning itself on a rock. Your sister tells everyone to stay perfectly still, then she picks up a large stick, slowly makes her way to the snake, and kills it.**
What Do You Think?
   - your sister was right to kill the snake because it was poisonous
   - your sister shouldn't have killed the snake because the snake was sunning itself; but if the snake looked as if it might strike she would have been right to kill it
   - all of you should have tried to walk away without harming the snake
   - your sister was right to kill the snake because it's OK to kill any snake if it gets too close to people
   - other

63

4. **You and your family visit a roadside zoo that advertised an exhibit featuring live snakes and other herps. After paying $3.00 a person to get inside, you see that the exhibits are falling apart and the reptiles are poorly cared for. Many of the animals have no water, and others are crammed together in tiny cages. In one of the cages, a dead snake is in the corner. And the turtle tank is filthy.**

What Would You Do?

- ask to see the owner and explain how upset you are about the conditions
- not say anything because you don't want to make the people that are working there feel bad
- ask for your money back and leave
- think about it and eventually call or write a letter to an animal protection organization
- not say anything because the people who run the zoo know more about taking care of herps than you do
- other

5. **While on vacation in a foreign country, your mother decides to buy a pair of sunglasses with tortoise-shell frames. You remember reading that many sea turtles are endangered. But you're not sure that these frames were made from an endangered turtle.**

What Would You Do?

- ask your mother not to buy the glasses, just in case
- ask your mother not to buy the glasses, because you don't think it's right to make glasses from turtles whether they're endangered or not
- ask the salesperson if the frames are from an endangered turtle, and if he or she says no, tell your mother it's OK
- let your mother decide for herself what she should do
- other

6. **Every year, thousands of garter snakes hibernate in caves in Manitoba's lake region in Canada. In spring, as the garter snakes emerge, collectors from all over North America stand outside the dens, waiting to capture them. The collectors sell the snakes to supply companies and pet stores. Over the years, the number of dens has decreased from 100 to about 30, and scientists are worried that the snake populations are in trouble.**

What Do You Think?

- it's OK to collect the snakes because many are being used in schools to educate people
- it's OK to collect some snakes, but the number of snakes collected should be regulated
- there should be laws to prohibit all snake collecting for profit
- other

7. **Your next door neighbor takes a trip to India and brings back presents for your family. She gives you a belt made from the skin of an Indian snake.**

What Would You Do?

- thank her but tell her you can't accept the gift because you think the belt could have been made from an endangered snake
- thank her and take the belt, even though it might have been made from an endangered snake; later talk to her about products made from endangered animals so she's not likely to buy such things in the future
- get angry with her for buying a product made with snakeskin, and tell her she shouldn't have bought something if it even had a chance of coming from an endangered animal
- thank her and wear the belt because you'd be the only person with such a neat belt
- other

Masks That Zap!

Luise Woelflein

Make a colorful chameleon or frog mask.

Ages:
Intermediate

Materials:
- white paper plates
- paper egg cartons
- scissors
- pencils
- paper punch
- paper party blowouts
- glue
- markers or paints and paintbrushes
- string or yarn
- pictures of chameleons and frogs

Subjects:
Arts and Crafts

shape mask like this for a frog

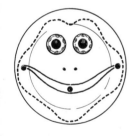

shape mask like this for a chameleon

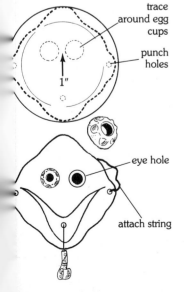

trace around egg cups

punch holes

1"

eye hole

attach string

Your kids will have fun making and wearing chameleon and frog masks that have workable "tongues." Before you begin, show the kids pictures of some real frogs and chameleons. Then follow these steps to make the masks:

1. Cut the sides of a paper plate to look like a chameleon or frog face (see diagram). *Note:* To make it easier for the kids, you might want to make patterns for them to trace around.

2. Make the eyes by cutting out two egg cups from a paper egg carton. Trim them so that the edges are round and even. Then poke scissors through the bottom of each cup and cut out a circle about ¾ inches (2 cm) wide.

3. Place the egg cups (bottoms facing up) in the center of the mask about one inch (2.5 cm) apart (see diagram). Trace around each one. Then cut out holes that are about ¼ inch (6 mm) smaller than the circles you traced. Finally, glue the egg cups in place over the holes you just cut and let dry.

4. To figure out where the "tongue" (i.e., the party blowout) goes, first sketch in the mouth on the front of your mask. Then place the mouthpiece of the party blowout on the mask where you want the tongue to be. (Make sure it lines up with your mouth!) Trace around the mouthpiece and then cut out the circle.

5. Use markers or paints to decorate your mask.

6. Punch a hole on each side of the mask and tie one piece of string or yarn to each hole. To wear the mask, have someone tie the two strings together in back of your head. Adjust the knot so that you're able to slip the mask on and off easily.

7. Put your mask on, and slip the mouthpiece of the party blowout through the hole. Now you're ready to zap any unsuspecting "bugs," or maybe just your unsuspecting friends!

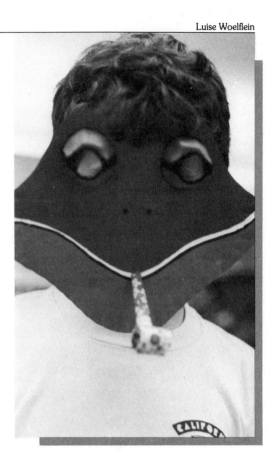

Make a Slinky Snake

Use toilet paper rolls and paper fasteners to make a movable snake.

Ages:
Advanced

Materials:
- *toilet paper rolls*
- *scissors*
- *paper punches*
- *paper fasteners*
- *thin cardboard or manila folders*
- *tape*
- *crayons, markers, or paint and paintbrushes*
- *pictures of snakes*

Subjects:
Arts and Crafts

Your kids can make a movable snake that will wrap around their arms and slither across the floor. Just have them follow these easy steps:

1. Cut five toilet paper rolls into fifteen 1½-inch (4-cm) long pieces. (These will be the snake's body segments.)
2. Cut two side notches in each end of thirteen of the pieces. The notches should be about ¼ to ½ inch (.6-1.3 cm) deep and 1 inch (2.5 cm) wide (see diagram 1). Then punch four holes in each segment as shown in the diagram.
3. Make end pieces by cutting two side notches in just one end of the two remaining segments. Then punch two holes in each of these segments (see diagram 2).
4. Starting with an end piece, assemble the body segments one by one. Fit the pieces together as shown in diagram 3. Then insert paper fasteners into the holes and spread the ends of the fasteners apart inside the snake. (Be sure to fit the cardboard pieces together as shown in the diagram. And

don't fasten the paper fasteners too tight or your snake will not be able to move easily.)

5. To make the head, cut out a 5 × 6-inch (13 × 15-cm) piece of thin cardboard or manila folder and roll it into a tube. (The tube should be slightly wider than the toilet paper roll.) Fit one end of the tube over one of the end segments and tape the edges of the tube together. Then tape the head to the end segment and cut out the snake's mouth (see diagram 5).
6. Cut out a forked tongue from the cardboard and tape it inside the snake's mouth.
7. To make a tail, cut out a 5 × 6-inch (13 × 15-cm) piece of cardboard and roll it into a cone. Tape the cone together and then trim off the top so that it's even (see diagram 4). Fit the larger end over the other end segment and tape it in place (see diagram 5).
8. Use crayons, markers, or paints to decorate the snake. (Provide pictures of snakes for the kids so they can decorate their snakes accurately.)

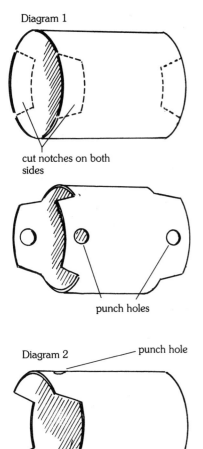

Diagram 1

cut notches on both sides

punch holes

Diagram 2

punch hole

cut notch

finished end piece

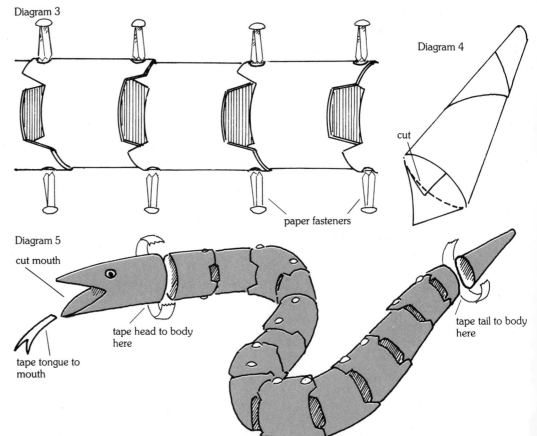

Diagram 3

paper fasteners

Diagram 4

cut

Diagram 5

cut mouth

tape head to body here

tape tongue to mouth

tape tail to body here

1997 Update

Table of Contents

INTRODUCTION TO HERP CARE

A mong pet owners, dogs and cats will probably always be tops, outranking all others. But lately, cuddly and furry creatures have been getting some real competition from scaly ones—reptiles. In just the past couple of years, snakes, turtles, and lizards have begun to play an important role in the pet trade.

This is partly because a growing number of veterinarians across the country are recommending reptiles over dogs and cats as pets for younger children. There are several reasons for this. Reptiles, or "exotics," as they are sometimes called, are just as interesting, cost less to maintain, and are often easier to care for than dogs and cats. Also, they don't cause allergies.

Caring for a low-maintenance reptile helps teach a young person responsibility. At the same time, because not much work is involved, it can be a positive learning experience. Growing tired of a pet because it needs too much care is a negative experience, unfortunate for both pet and owner.

Another reason reptiles are being adopted is that more and more vets are extending their services beyond traditional pets to the exotics. This is quite different from just a few years ago when getting treatment for a sick snake or injured iguana was generally difficult, if not impossible.

Now, with medical care and printed information about reptiles more readily available, larger numbers of pet owners are choosing to adopt this type of animal, one that lives in an aquarium or cage and doesn't need the high-level care of a dog or cat.

In fact, interest has grown so much over the past three years that retail sales of reptiles, or "herps," have risen 38 percent. Last year, pet owners spent more than $30 million to buy them.

Herps, which are "ectotherms," meaning cold-blooded, may not be warm and cuddly, but they make excellent pets for many reasons. Best of all, with proper care, many species can live a lot longer than cats or dogs, some of them 50 or more years! Most herps also are fairly low-maintenance and don't need daily walks or even daily attention. Therefore, they fit easily into an owner's busy schedule.

Reptiles are also less expensive to keep. Unlike dogs and cats, they don't need inoculations (unless they become ill), and they eat much less food. In fact, once they've grown out of the juvenile stage, when frequent feedings are necessary for proper growth and good health, many snakes and turtles don't need to eat more than once a week. And certain snakes, when full grown, eat just once a month! This, too, means less work for the owner: While the cage does need to be cleaned occasionally, it doesn't need to be done often.

Because they don't need a lot of care, certain reptiles make a good choice of pet for young people with little or no experience. But there are so many to choose from! Which ones make the best pets? Choosing the right animal is important.

DON'TS

First, there are herps no beginner should ever buy and, in fact, many communities have passed laws prohibiting people from keeping dangerous reptiles. If

68

pet owners have any doubts about the legality of a pet they plan to buy, they should check with the proper authorities.

Among the herps that should not be kept are the crocodilians—alligator, crocodile, caiman, or gavial. They might look adorable when they're small, but they don't make good pets and should not be handled by anyone who isn't properly trained.

Crocodilians should be thought of as "hunting machines" that don't tame down or become friendly, even to their owner. And little pleasure can be gotten from owning a "pet" that can't be handled, or one that can cause severe injury or worse.

Venomous snakes also are poor choices for pets. (People often make the mistake of calling venomous snakes "poisonous." The fact is, you can bite them and not get sick. But you will get sick if a venomous snake bites you!)

Snakes in general are clever escape artists, and a venomous snake on the loose poses a serious threat not only to its owner, but also to the owner's family and even the neighbors. The least dangerous venomous snake is the copperhead, but a bite can cost the victim a finger.

Other herps not recommended as pets are large constrictors such as Burmese pythons; reticulated or African rock pythons; and anacondas, snakes that can grow up to 30 feet long (the average is about 15 feet). *Any* snake longer than 6 or 8 feet can be unmanageable and dangerous.

Many lizard species make excellent pets but some don't, among them the venomous Gila monster and beaded lizard. These, like the other animals mentioned above, should be left either in the wild or in the care of trained handlers.

Turtles, box turtles or water turtles, and tortoises, with dozens of interesting species available, are good choices for pet owners who have some experience, because they require a fairly high level of care. The same goes for monitors, iguanas, and chameleons—they're great pets but not for beginners.

DO'S

By now readers know a lot of "don'ts" about choosing a reptile for a pet. Now about the "do's." The best choices for new owners, young people who want a low-maintenance pet (and don't want to be nagged to take care of it!), are bearded dragons, leopard geckos, kingsnakes or corn snakes, and boa constrictors. But remember, although these animals don't need a lot of care, there are certain basics that they must have: proper housing, diet, and temperature.

Leopard gecko (Eublepharis macularius): its bright colors, unagressive behavior, and ease of care make it an ideal first pet for the young collector. The Latin means "eyelid" and "spotted." They are native to Afganistan, North India, and Pakistan. Adults reach 8 to 12 inches in length.

Bearded dragons, which are native to Australia, were hardly known in this country as recently as seven or eight years ago but are now quite popular. (Australians refer to several of their lizard species as "dragon.")

These animals stay fairly small, never growing longer than two feet, including the tail. They're friendly creatures, attractive and docile, and can be handled for short periods of time. They do require some daily care but not a lot.

Pet stores usually charge between $90 and $125 for a young bearded dragon, $125 to $150 for an adult male, and as much as $300 for an adult female.

Bearded dragons can be kept either as individuals or in small groups. For one animal, a 20-gallon aquarium makes a good *vivarium* (container for land-dwelling reptiles), and a 30-gallon tank provides plenty of space for up to three animals.

The lizard's tank should include a *substrate* (material placed on the floor of the vivarium), a full-spectrum light, a hot spot for basking, a branch to crawl on, and a water bowl (the bowl is optional, as bearded dragons don't drink if they're fed properly).

Playground sand works best for the substrate, but make sure it's not silica, which can clump and constipate the animal. Ask about this at the pet store and always read the package. Red desert sand is attractive and also a good choice, as are aspen shavings or newspaper.

A full-spectrum fluorescent bulb, including ultraviolet (UV), is necessary for the animal's body to produce Vitamin D. (Make sure the bulb is labeled full-spectrum, because a regular fluorescent bulb does not provide UV.)

Like all pet reptiles, bearded dragons need a basking area or hot spot during the day, and they need darkness at night. To make sure the vivarium temperature is right, a new owner needs to rely on a thermometer.

The coolest area in the tank should be about 80° Fahrenheit. The hot spot, which can be provided by a silver-domed reflector lamp, should stay between 90 and 95 degrees. Light bulb wattage will vary according to the time of year, but a 60- or 75-watt bulb usually works well.

Important: The bearded dragon (or any reptile) must be able to escape from the heat if it chooses, because overheating can quickly be fatal.

Hot rocks, which can malfunction and burn the animal, are not recommended. There are better choices, ones that provide a habitat closer to nature (such as heating the animal from above). And that's the basis of good animal care, or husbandry: making the captive conditions as much like the animal's natural setting as possible.

Bearded dragons are easy to please when it comes to food. Their diet should consist of 6 to 12 live crickets apiece daily and a "salad" of greens every other day. The most wholesome are collard and mustard greens, or red lettuce (not iceberg lettuce, which has little food value).

Don't feed spinach and broccoli as these prevent calcium from being absorbed, which the animals' bodies need, and contain a type of salt that can damage their kidneys. Also avoid feeding kale and cabbage (though few reptiles show much interest in cabbage), as these can cause thyroid problems.

Both greens and crickets should be supplemented with powdered vitamins and minerals, most importantly calcium. This is available at pet stores. Feed the powder by adding half a teaspoon to a plastic bag that contains the greens or crickets, and shake gently to coat.

Leopard geckos, which were the first lizards to be commercially "produced" on a large scale, also make excellent pets, and their care is similar to that of the bearded dragon.

Pet shops generally charge between $45 and $55 for a young gecko two or three inches long (leopard geckos grow to about eight inches and, with proper care, can live 25 to 30 years).

Leopard geckos are not aggressive animals and seldom bite (even if they do, the bite doesn't amount to much). They are not overly fond of being handled, but the more the owner does handle them, the calmer they will be. (Never pick up a gecko, or any lizard, by the tail, as it will frighten and may even injure it.)

Like bearded dragons, geckos can be kept as individuals or in groups made up of several females but only one male. This is important, as males housed together will fight.

A 10-gallon tank makes a roomy vivarium for one gecko, and up to six females and one male will do well in a 20-gallon tank. A lid isn't necessary but is recommended if the family includes young children, cats, or dogs.

Playground sand or red desert sand can be the substrate, and a "hide box" should be provided. This can be as simple as a cardboard box big enough for all the animals to crawl inside with one side cut away. Vivarium and hot spot temperatures should be the same as for the bearded dragon.

Geckos also eat live crickets, three to six a day, and need the calcium supplement once a week. Geckos enjoy an occasional wax worm. Don't feed meal worms that can clog the lower digestive track and result in a trip to the vet; an inexperienced pet owner should never try to doctor a pet.

A live pinky mouse can be offered once a week for a treat. Like many animals, geckos are "motion oriented" and won't eat anything that doesn't move!

Also remember that crickets need to eat. If you keep them to feed your herp, provide them with slices of orange or carrot, a little skin of yellow squash or sections of yams.

Caring for the vivarium is easy. Leopard geckos are clean animals that always defecate in the same area. Their stools are dry and easy to scoop out and will need to be removed only about every two weeks. The vivarium must be kept dry, with no spilled water. When water mixes with the uric acid of the animal's feces, ammonia is produced, which is lethal to geckos.

Another excellent beginner's pet is the red-tailed boa, a species com-

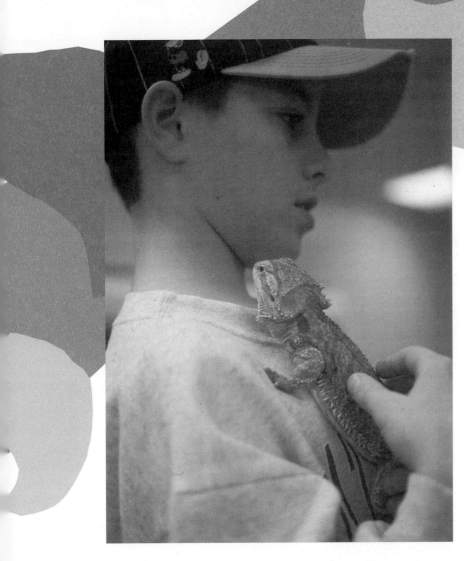

mon in the wild all over South America. These are the best choice of the dozen or more boa species, as the others need more specialized care and may be less docile.

A baby red-tailed boa sells for between $90 and $125 at pet shops, and the setup costs between $75 and $100 more. Captive-bred animals are a little more expensive but are a far better choice than wild-caught animals. Those bred in captivity tend to have fewer internal parasites or disease-causing organisms and in general are healthier.

Also, captive-bred animals don't suffer while adapting to captivity, have better dispositions, and are easier to handle. All reputable pet shops will tell buyers whether an animal is captive-bred. Any imported (wild-caught) boa should have its stool checked for parasites by a qualified vet.

Be prepared for the pet boa to grow quickly. A youngster 12 to 15 inches long can, if cared for properly, grow to 7 feet within a year. With good care, the boa can live 10 to 15 years (occasionally they live as long as 40 years).

A 20-gallon tank—with a secure lid!—makes a good vivarium for a young boa, but larger quarters must be provided as the animal grows. Again, the most important piece of equipment is a thermometer. The boa's tank, like those of the bearded dragon and leopard gecko, should be kept at 80 degrees with a daytime hot spot at 90 to 95 degrees. Temperatures should be checked several times each day. If you are gone during the day, turn on the light in the morning, check the temperature, and make sure the animal can escape light at one end in a hide box.

Boas need a water bowl that they can't overturn, preferably one of ceramic or metal. They also need a branch or rocks to climb on.

The substrate can be newspaper, which will need to be changed once or twice a

Handling the dragon on a regular basis, along with hand feeding, can lead to a close relationship with it. While bearded dragons are not skittish and seem to enjoy regular handling, you must remember that they can suddenly dart from their perch and escape. Consequently, handling should be done in a closed area (like a room with the door shut) and for short periods.

week for young boas, and once or twice a month for adults. Astroturf or aspen shavings also work well, but don't use aspen *chips* because they can puncture the animal's bowel. A snake can be hurt if it ingests small material such as bark, mulch, rocks, gravel, or chips. If you use these, you should feed the snake outside the vivarium.

A very young boa should be fed small mice frozen or thawed. As it grows, the size of the prey should also increase, first to rats, then rabbits, and finally chickens, with the width of the prey not larger than that of the snake at its midsection. Freshly killed or thawed frozen prey are best both for humane reasons and the safety of the snake.

As a general rule, a boa up to three feet long should be fed one or two mice every four or five days; between three and six feet long, one or two rats every five to seven days; and six feet and larger, one or two rabbits or chickens every week to ten days.

Several important things to remember when feeding a large boa constrictor include keeping just one snake per cage; only one gets fed at a time. Also, move the snake away from the cage door with a stick or a rod before opening it, and toss the prey in—never hold it until the snake strikes to grab it. If the snake doesn't eat the prey, for safety's sake use long tongs to remove it.

Kingsnakes and corn snakes are beautiful animals and make excellent pets for beginners. Kingsnakes cost between $45 and $80; corn snakes, between $25 and $50. If possible have a vet check the animal before you buy it. All snakes should be well rounded, with no ribs showing, and have good muscle tone. There should be no mucus in the mouth (a sign of respiratory infection), no mouth rot, lumps, mites, or ticks.

The habitat requirements for kingsnakes and corn snakes are about the same as for a boa. A ten-gallon aquarium will work for a hatchling, with a larger tank needed as the snake grows. A hide box should be provided, as should a water bowl, hot spot, and branch for climbing. Several corn snakes can be housed together, but—and this is important--kingsnakes, which are snake eaters, cannot!

Hatchling snakes should be fed pinky mice, one every two to five days. Again, the size of the prey should increase as the snake grows, but corn snakes and kingsnakes do well their entire life (10 to 15 years) eating only mice, preferably thawed frozen (don't use the microwave for thawing as it will cook the meat).

To provide the best possible care for any animal, new owners should learn everything they can about their pet. This means buying booklets, generally inexpensive, which many vets and pet stores sell, and reading them thoroughly. A well-cared-for pet reptile will live a long time and provide lots of enjoyment.

Answers to Copycat Page—
Herp Care (p.75)

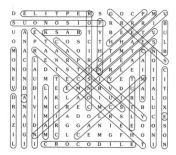

Books to Read
Ball Pythons: Their Captive Husbandry and Reproduction by Jon Coote (1996)
The General Care and Maintenance of Bearded Dragons by Philippe De Vosjoli and Robert Mailloux (1993)
The General Care and Maintenance of Burmese Pythons by Philippe De Vosjoli (1991)
The General Care and Maintenance of Common Kingsnakes by David Perlowin (1991)
The General Care and Maintenance of Leopard Geckos and African Fat-tailed Geckos by Philippe De Vosjoli (1990)
The General Care and Maintenance of Red-Tailed Boas by Philippe De Vosjoli (1990)
Keeping and Breeding Corn Snakes by Michael J. McEachern (1991)
Practical Encyclopedia of Keeping and Breeding Tortoises and Freshwater Turtles by A.C. Highfield (1996)
Information for this story was also provided by: Daniel Wentz, DVM, Ferguson Animal Clinic, St. Louis, MO., Ron Goellner, General Curator (former Curator of Reptiles), St. Louis Zoo., Frank Pusateri, DVM, Stonegate Animal Hospital, Valley Park, MO.

HERP CARE

ANACONDA
BASK
BULB
CAIMAN
CALCIUM
CAPTIVITY
CONSTRICTOR
CRICKET
CROCODILE
ECTOTHERM
EXOTIC
GREENS
HERP
IGUANA
INDIVIDUAL

INOCULATION
LIFE
LIZARD
MAMMAL
NOSE
POISONOUS
PYTHON
REPTILE
SCALY
SUBSTRATE
THERMOMETER
TURTLE
VENOM
VETERINARIAN
VITAMIN

```
D E L I T P E R S G O C P M V
S U O N O S I O P R R R R I B
U A E K S A B T Y B E E T V U
O N P T C O S C T H H A E S L
M A R A A A O I H T M T C N B
O C L E N R P R O I E A A O S
N O A D T S T T N R L E I I C
E N U M T E C S I Y E T M T I
V D D L E E M N B V D U A A T
D A I A K L A O I U I R N L O
R N V M C R E C M C S T B U X
A A I M I A D O L R S L Y C E
Z U D A R G G A N I E E O O S
I G N M C L C E M G F H O N O
L I I C R O C O D I L E T I N
```

EXTINCTION EXERCISE

ALLIGATOR
BURROW
CONSERVATION
ENDANGERED
GENE
HUMAN
INTRODUCED
RESOURCES
SEA TURTLE
TERRITORY
VULNERABLE

BIODIVERSITY
CHAIN REACTION
DARWIN
EXTIRPATED
HAWKSBILL
INDIGENOUS
PROTECTION
SAVE
SNAKE
THREATENED
WILDLIFE

```
I I N T R O D U C E D J U N G
M H S D N O I T C E T O R P S
E W U U E I W O R R U B C R E
D Y N M O S W E N V U H B L C
E E A O A N G R U R A I T S R
T S N V I N E L A I O R O H U
A N E E A T N G N D U L A E O
P A E D T E A R I T E W L F S
R K N M R A E V A D K N L I E
I E C A O A E E R S N E I L R
T S B I C R S R B E N I G D O
X L D T S M I I H I S E A L O
E C I I I A L V W T N N T I M
I O T D L L B R N E L T O W E
N Y Y R O T I R R E T T R C D
```

AN EXTINCT REPTILE IS GONE FOREVER

E xtinct means gone forever." How often we hear those words from conservationists, scientists and just concerned individuals! These people worry that populations of certain animal species, some of them reptiles, are shrinking and may one day disappear from the earth altogether. The death of an entire species is called "extinction."

HOW DO ANIMALS BECOME EXTINCT?

Animal populations die off for various reasons. One theory is that an older species may find itself competing with a newer species, one that has recently evolved, for a particular ecological *niche* (habitat that supports it). Both species may eat the same food, and the food may be limited in supply. If the newer species is better at gathering food, it will thrive and the older species may eventually die out because it can't compete successfully in that environment.

Juvenile alligator snapper

Extinction of a species has happened—generally slowly—millions of times. But today, man is accelerating the process, killing off species by moving into and altering animal habitats. Human populations are growing almost everywhere, and people need—or think they need—to fill the space animals occupy. Man has a larger, more highly developed brain than any other creature on earth, and this has enabled him to take over nearly every environment.

We all have seen, probably often, what happens when animals are forced out of their habitat. In the niche they occupy in a particular ecosystem, the food and shelter they need is available. But when land is cleared to make way for new homes or an office building or highway, that ecosystem is changed in ways that can no longer support the wildlife that lived there. As trees, brush, and rocks that provided shelter are bulldozed away, a chain reaction begins. Small plants, animals, and insects die; then animals that eat them die; and finally the animals that eat the animals that eat the small plants, animals, and insects die. All this happens because, without food sources, the land cannot sustain wild animals.

Many of these animals have nowhere else to go. Unable to find a suitable new territory, they will likely starve to death or otherwise be killed, the direct result of their loss of habitat. Herpetologists tell us, for instance, that so many displaced ornate and common box turtles get killed every year that they are now considered "near threatened," which means that their numbers are declining so rapidly that they could eventually become endangered.

Adult alligator snapping turtle. These large snappers often weigh more than 100 pounds. Their hunting method is called "passive." They lie at the bottom of shallow ponds so they can breathe simply by extending their neck and lifting their head to the surface. They stay very quiet until fish swim close, then slowly open their mouth and show a pink worm-like "lure" on the floor of their mouth. When the fish swims in to take the bait, it's dinner time. Prized for their meat, alligator snappers have been hunted in the South for years. Now the season is limited and hunters can't take young or "juvenile" animals, and the alligator snapper may make a comeback.

SEA TURTLES AND PYTHONS

Other reptiles have fared worse. Sea turtle populations have been severely depleted by unthinking people who kill adult and juvenile turtles, and even those still in the egg. It's against the law, but poachers often loot nests of the round white eggs and eat them, believing—wrongly—that they have unusual medicinal properties.

Sea turtles, especially over the past 50 years, have been killed in huge numbers for their meat; the skin on their flippers for leather; their shells for jewelry or crafts; or the whole animal, which is stuffed and hung on the wall for decoration.

For years, Japan alone imported enough hawksbill sea turtles annually—36,000 or more—to ultimately drive the animals to extinction had the mass killings continued. Fortunately, Japan finally gave in to world pressure and agreed to stop importing the endangered hawksbills in 1993. Because enough people cared and worked to stop the exploitation of these turtles, it's possible the species can recover.

Reticulated pythons, large, ornately patterned snakes that live in the dry jungles of Southeast Asia and nearby Pacific islands, are also threatened by the leather trade. They, too, have suffered from loss of habitat, as have the strikingly beautiful black and yellow radiated tortoises once common on the African island of Madagascar. These animals are much sought after for their colorful shells and meat, and also for the exotic pet market. Today they're nearly gone from the wild.

But there may also be hope for this species. Illegal trading continues, but radiated tortoises are often seized by authorities, and these animals have become the stock of successful breeding programs.

THE GIANT TORTOISE

Among declining or extinct reptile populations, some of the most unfortunate are the giant tortoises that abounded centuries ago on the Galapagos Islands off the coast of Ecuador in South America. These tortoises not only differed from those on the mainland, but were also unique from island to island. Over many thousands of years, the tortoises had "adapted" to each island's different environment.

Until people came to Galapagos in the 16th century, the tortoises had no predators. Turtles and tortoises grow slowly throughout their entire lives. Thus, if nothing eats

The Western Desert Tortoise. Once found in large numbers throughout the Southwest, the desert tortoise, or Gopherus agassizii, was recently hunted to near extinction by cosmetic companies who used the turtle's natural oil in face cream. The gopher tortoises are named for their practice of living in long burrows (sometimes more than 30 feet). Along with its gopher turtle cousins in Florida, Texas, and Mexico, the desert tortoise today is either threatened or endangered over all of its range. Due to an airborne respiratory illness that seems to affect them, it may be impossible to save these beautiful creatures.

them, they eventually grow quite large. Depending on which island they call home, adult Galapagos tortoises can weigh from 150 to 600 pounds.

For centuries, the docile tortoises lived at peace with other animals on the islands. Their end began when sailors—pirates, whalers, and sealers—started coming ashore in search of food; and the tortoises, like other Galapagos animal species, didn't realize they had anything to fear.

Heavy and slow-moving, the tortoises were easy prey. Over the next three centuries, they were captured by the hundreds and taken on board ships. Tortoises, unlike most animals, can live many months without food or water and could be stacked up in a ship's hold as an ongoing source of food, oil, and even water, which their bodies store.

By the time laws were finally passed to protect these magnificent animals, more than 100,000 had been killed. Sad to say, even scientific expeditions killed many of them.

The tortoises of Galapagos are now protected as endangered species, and breeding programs are underway, but fewer than 15,000 individuals remain. Originally they lived on ten of the Galapagos islands. Today they are found on only six.

More recently, before they were also protected, tortoises in the United States suffered just as badly. The desert tortoises of the Southwest and gopher tortoises of the Southeast were nearly wiped out for their oil. Hundreds of thousands of the animals were loaded into trailers and shipped to cosmetic companies to be slaughtered for women's face cream.

American alligators were hunted nearly to extinction for their hides and meat before federal protection 30 years ago encouraged their numbers to come back. Rattlesnakes may never make the endangered species list, but cruel roundups and slaughters every year in several Western states kill huge numbers of them.

Alligator snapping turtles, found in varying numbers in most of the states in the lower Mississippi River Valley, have also been widely hunted for their tasty meat. Today they're protected in nearly every state where they occur, but it could be too late. Recovery will not come quickly for the alligator snapper, and it could still disappear.

These are just a few cases in which humans, during the four million or so years they have lived on earth, have greatly harmed the reptiles and other animals that share the planet. Humanity might even be called a "catastrophe." And as the years go by, hu-

Answers to Copycat Page—
Extinction Exercise (p.75)

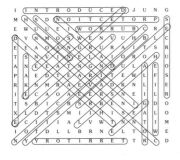

mans continue to damage the planet, extinguishing many of its species.

People want—and try hard—to alter the earth to suit their own needs and desires. In the process, they often forget that other species deserve their proper share.

Some people are now aware--and concerned--about the damage we are doing to the earth and its creatures, though it may be too late for some species. It's been estimated that the rate of extinction of animal populations between 1600 and 1975 was 5 to 50 times higher than it had been in earlier eons. That rate is projected to rise over the next few decades to 40 to 400 times more than "normal."

Charles Darwin, a biologist who developed the idea of evolution of species more than 100 years ago, believed that a natural evolutionary process had gone on for millions of years with no human participation. He believed in "natural selection," in which chance genetic mutations combine with factors in the environment to bring about the evolution of some species and the extinction of others. Darwin theorized that the success of some species is paid for by a shrinking in population size, or elimination, of others.

He believed this was natural, that the extinction of a whole species is as normal as the death of an individual animal. The death of individuals is inevitable, and so is extinction, even though a species may live for millions of years. But humans have raised the rate of species extinction, and now animals are disappearing more quickly than they are appearing. That rate promises to keep accelerating.

Should we be concerned about the growing imbalance between the rate of extinction and rate of species creation? Should we care about every disappearing species? Yes we should, because every animal, however small, is an important part of life on earth.

Spiny softshell turtle. This turtle, photographed on a Florida roadside, is in the process of digging its nest. Although the softshell turtle isn't endangered, this practice shows why so many turtles are. Often slow and unthreatening, turtles lay their eggs in places vulnerable to egg poaching. Egg thieves, especially of sea turtle eggs that are laid in a similar way, often take all the eggs, leaving none to carry on the species. Decades of this practice can leave a turtle species on the edge of extinction.

Some environmentalists argue that we must draw the line to end destruction and not only because our own fates are intertwined with those of the animals who share the planet. Some say that a long-standing existence carries with it the right to continue living. Many say that people should not have the right to decide which species live and which ones die.

Scientists tell us that, world-wide, about 250 species of reptiles are now considered threatened. Nearly half of the 23 species of crocodilians—crocodiles, alligators, caimans, and gavials—are threatened. These numbers are shocking, but although some species keep decreasing in numbers, crocodilians are one of the few orders of threatened animals whose status has improved in the past 20 years. This is thanks to conservation efforts taken in time to save them.

Of the many tortoise, turtle, and terrapin species around the world, more than one-third are considered threatened. Another one-fifth are near-threatened. All species of sea turtles are threatened.

It might surprise us to learn that the countries with the most threatened reptile species are Australia, with 37, and the United States, with 28. South Africa and Indonesia are close behind with 19 threatened reptile species each, Mexico with 17, and China with 15. Over the past 400 years, 20 reptile species have become extinct (compared with 104 bird species and 86 mammal species wiped out during those same four centuries).

What can we do?

There are steps that can be taken to prevent other threatened or endangered reptile species from disappearing. Sea turtles, for instance, can be saved from the nets of shrimp fishermen, where they generally drown, with a device called a "turtle excluder" that enables the animals to escape. Many shrimpers, who scoop up the turtles along with thousands of pounds of unwanted fish while gathering shrimp, say the excluders are expensive and they don't want to use them.

Another way to save sea turtles is to protect their nests on the sandy beaches of the

Apache Junction, Arizona. In the spectacular setting at the foot of the Superstition Mountains outside Phoenix, Apache Junction is an example of how people take over a delicate environment, in this case Southwestern desert, and develops it for their own use with little regard for the plants and animals that evolved here. People can live almost anywhere on earth because they can use their intellect to change an existing environment to fit their needs. The problem is that after the environment has been changed, plants and animals that have taken many years to adapt are left homeless. Unlike people, the plants and animals cannot move elsewhere and adapt a new home to suit them. They simply die.

Gulf of Mexico where the females come ashore to lay. They can also be saved through programs in which eggs are carefully removed from nests and incubated in safety. A film made 50 years ago showed about 40,000 females ashore laying eggs on a Mexican beach. In 1990, only 350 females were seen on that same beach. Clearly, without protection, sea turtles won't be around much longer.

But people, who have caused many of the problems that endanger the earth's wildlife species, can also help. We can decide not to buy anything that comes from an endangered species, things such as lizard or snake skin leather, tortoise shell jewelry, stuffed sea turtles or turtle oil cosmetics. We can refuse to buy reptile body parts. (Alligator heads, alligator snapping turtle skulls, and caiman feet are sometimes seen for sale.)

We can leave animals alone when we see them in the wild (unless a turtle needs to be moved to safety off a road, or has been injured and can be helped by a veterinarian and later released). We can refuse to buy any wild--caught or endangered reptile for a pet. If there is no market for these animals, the illegal trade will end, and the species may survive.

We can be careful how we dispose of our trash. Instead of throwing it away, we should recycle everything we can. Landfills consume animal habitats, and plastic bags, six-pack can holders, and other items can injure or kill reptiles, and fish that swallow or get caught in them.

We can contribute and encourage others to contribute to organizations that buy habitat to protect endangered species and ecosystems.

Thomas Jefferson, our third president and a renowned naturalist wrote, ". . . if one link in nature's chain might be lost, another and another might be lost, till this whole system of things should vanish by piecemeal."

If enough people care and take part, the threatened and endangered reptile species of today may survive to be a thriving part of our wildlife heritage tomorrow.

Two Origami Jumping Frogs

Decorate your classroom with these fabulous folded frogs, designed for two different skill levels (with 1=easy and 2=more difficult). Use these from K-12 as art projects and as math projects from K-6.

Frog One

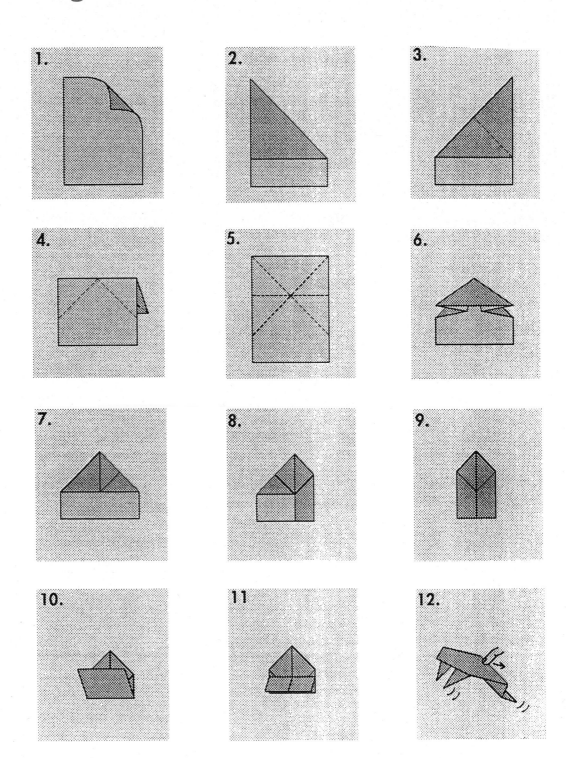

Frog Two

1. If you do not use the grain of the paper, the frog will not jump when finished.

2 and 3. Turn it over and fold.

4-6. Fold along the creases and make a triangle.

7. Fold as shown.

8. Fold the right and left edges to the center, without folding the top triangle.

9-10. Fold as shown.

11-13. Open up the pockets in the lower triangle and bring it up to the corners of the upper triangle.

14. Fold as shown.

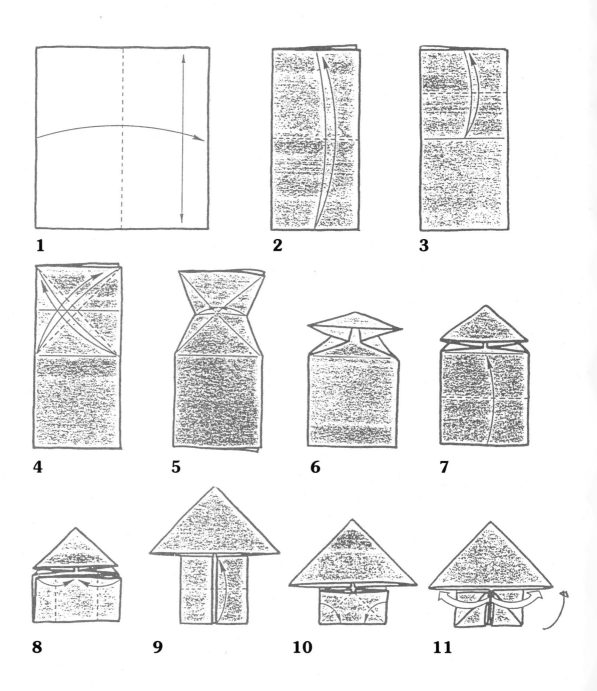

15. You have made four legs now. Fold in half where the legs meet.

16. Fold the upper edge down a little. Do not fold half-way

17. Turn it over.

18. Finished!

These designs are based on the work of the Nippon Origami Association, Tokyo, Japan. Deg Farrelly drew the sketches for Frog One. Frog Two is based on the drawings of the Sanrio Company. Walter Enloe contributed translations from the descriptions of Hisashi Abe.

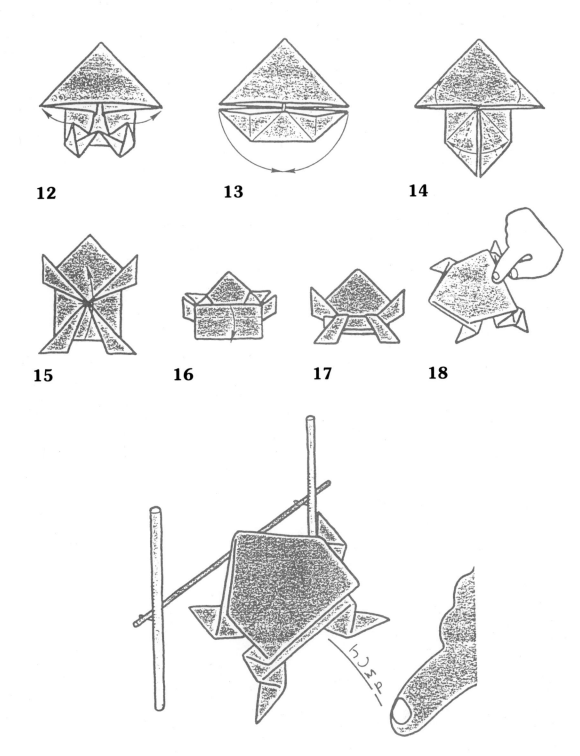

12   **13**   **14**

15   **16**   **17**   **18**

Metamorphosis for a Change

"How the Frog Lost Its Tail"

—a West African Folk Tale

Long, long ago when the world was new, Frog became miserable because he was the only creature in the water hole that didn't have a tail. When all the other animals came to drink, they proudly showed off their tails and made fun of Frog.

So Frog gathered up his courage and begged Nyame, the Sky God, to give him a tail. Nyame agreed, but in return she asked Frog to be the keeper of her own special well that never dried up. Frog promised to share the water with all the other animals.

It wasn't long before Frog became very conceited about his long, beautiful tail and got very bossy about who could share the water at the Sky God's well.

When the other wells dried up during a drought, Frog was rude, shouting at the other animals "Go away! There is no water here."

Nyame was very unhappy when she heard of Frog's behavior. She disguised herself and came to the well to drink. When Frog treated her very unkindly, Nyame became angry and decided Frog must be punished. She took away Frog's tail and banished him from the well.

From then on, Nyame gave all newborn frogs a beautiful tail, but caused their tails to disappear gradually as they grew. And that is how it is to this very day.

The development of a frog begins in the early spring. Adult frogs migrate from their deeper wintering lakes, where predators become active as the water temperature warms. They find shallow breeding ponds safe from predators in which to lay their eggs. The male climbs on the female's back and uses his muscular front legs to squeeze her around the middle, causing her to lay as many as 6,500 eggs into the water. The male then fertilizes the eggs.

The jelly-like eggs can often be seen clinging to pond plants. The eggs separate and grow, hatching into tadpoles in 6 to 14 days. Tadpoles feed on algae. They have gills and breathe like fish. After about seven weeks the tadpoles begin to change to froglets as hind legs appear. At about 12 weeks, the tadpole's tail shrinks, lungs develop, and jaws replace algae-feeding discs. By week 14, froglets can breathe air and leave the water. As fully developed frogs, they feed on moving insects such as earthworms, crickets, and grasshoppers. They have long, sticky tongues to catch their prey.

ACTIVITY

1. Read the story in the sidebar "How The Frog Lost Its Tail"—a West African Folk Tale. Be sure that students understand that folk tales are not meant to be factual.
2. Use a book such as *The Tadpole* by Hidetomo Odo, to introduce, review, or reinforce the concept of metamorphosis.
3. Have students demonstrate their understanding of metamorphosis in one of the following ways:
- sequence pictures of a frog's development and write sentences to describe each stage.
- use the pictures or create hand puppets to tell other students or parents how metamorphosis in frogs occurs.

- research another creature that undergoes metamorphosis and illustrate the process.
- create a pond diorama including metamorphosis.
- use movement to act out the metamorphosis of a frog. Add music such as "Jeremiah was a Bullfrog" or other frog songs.
- write a story from the perspective of a frog, describing what is happening during the change from an egg to a tadpole to a frog.
- create a flip book of frog development. Illustrate each stage of development on 3 x 5 inch cards. Staple together and flip to see the action.

DISCUSSION

1. What did you like about the folk tale? In what other creative ways could we explain why Frog has no tail?
2. How is the development of frogs different from the development of humans? Why is human development not metamorphosis?

3. What might happen if a frog laid her eggs in a rain puddle?
4. What might happen to a frog egg if the water was suddenly polluted by a dangerous chemical such as bleach?

A Frog Natural History

This exercise provides students and teachers with an opportunity to explore the amazing frog diversity to be found in the United States and the rest of the world. The map on page 86 gives you an introduction to at least one of the frogs in your area. Students should try to fill in their own areas with descriptions of other types of frogs that they might find on a frogging expedition. (Public libraries are usually excellent resources for field guides, hand books and picture books.) The following exercises are especially enjoyable in small groups.

Exercise 1: Up close and personal

Pick a frog from your state to study. Look in picture books and field guides to see what you can learn about your frog. How does your frog defend itself? What does it look like? What does its call sound like? Where does it live? Draw a picture and report on your findings to the rest of the class.

Exercise 2: The frog awards

Search your library, web sites, or classroom resources for examples of frogs that you find interesting. You may limit your search to frogs of the United States, or you may include the entire world. Select contestants to receive awards in the following categories: strangest frog, most colorful, most interesting defensive strategy, and most unusual parental care methods. You may want to come up with some of your own categories as well. Older students can present top three candidates and classmates can vote in a mock election.

COPYCAT PAGE

Northern Wood Frog, or Cambridge Frog (Rana sylvatica).

This small frog is found in Alaska as well as parts of Canada, and northern parts of Minnesota, Michigan, and Wisconsin. It lives in woody areas among moss and dead leaves, moving to small ponds during breeding season. Its call is a scratchy "quack."
Males 36-50 mm and females 37-56 mm.

Northern Toad, or Mountain Toad, or Western Toad, or Baird's Toad (Bufo boreas).

This warty toad ranges all the way from Alaska to southwestern Utah and eastern Colorado. When not breeding, it can live in relatively dry habitats. One of its calls is a birdlike "chirp."
Males 56-108 mm and females 60-125 mm.

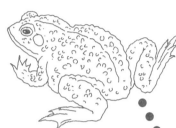

Narrow-mouthed Toad, Toothless Frog (Gastrophryne carolinensis).

This small, dark-colored frog is found in the Central United States, from Nebraska to Maryland, and south to Florida and Texas. It is a nocturnal frog that lives beneath decaying logs or leaves. The call is a loud, lamb-like "baa."
Males 20-34 mm and females 22-36 mm.

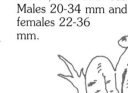

Leopard Frog (Rana pipiens).

This spotted frog is found in all states, except for Washington, Oregon, and California. In different parts of the country, the frog has different color patterns. Therefore, what we call the Leopard Frog may actually be many different frog species. The call is a low rumble, or snoring sound.
Males and females 50-90 mm.

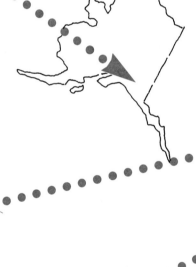

Canyon Tree Frog, Sonoran Tree Toad (Hyla arenicolor).

This chubby little frog is found throughout the Southwestern United States, all the way to Western Texas. With its large sticky toe pads, it clings to vertical canyon walls near clear flowing water. Its call is a low trill.
Males 29-53 mm and females 30-54 mm.

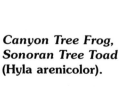

Great Plains Toad, Texas Toad, Western Toad (Bufo cognatus).

This stocky toad ranges through Texas and New Mexico north to the Dakotas. There is a dark-colored flap of skin under the throat that is visible only when calling. Its call is a scratchy, low-pitched trill.
Males 47-95 mm and females 60-99 mm.

A FROG NATURAL HISTORY

Spring Peeper, Striped Tree Frog, Swamp Cricket (Pseudacris triseriata).

This noisy frog ranges throughout the Great Lakes states and westward to Idaho. It is a drab animal, with a dark triangle or stripe between the eyes. Although a tree frog, it is mostly seen in low bushes and on the ground, moving to shallow ponds or ditches to breed. Its call is a shrill "peep." Males 21-32 mm and females 20-38 mm.

Common Tree Frog, Tree Toad, Changeable Tree Toad, Chameleon Hyla (Hyla versicolor).

This mid-sized frog is found throughout the entire eastern United States, with the exception of Southern Florida. It leaves small yellow eggs in clumps attached to aquatic vegetation, and remains in trees or mossy areas when not breeding. Its call is a loud trill. Males 32-51 mm and females 33-60 mm.

Bullfrog, American Bullfrog (Rana catesbeiana).

This is the largest frog in the United States, and can be found throughout the country, except for Southern Florida and the Dakotas. It is a solitary frog that is always in or near still water. The call has been described as a deep "jug-o-rum" sound, and is easily heard during early summer evenings. Males 85-180 mm and females 89-184 mm.

Cricket Frog, or Ricord's Frog, or Pink-snouted Frog (Eleutherodactylus ricordii).

This extremely small, delicate frog is found in Florida and may be spreading northward. Its size and a coral pink snout gives away the identity of this frog. Metamorphosis to adult form occurs in the egg, so there is no tadpole stage. The call is a faint "chirp," or "put-put." Males and females 15-30 mm.

Barking Frog, Georgia Tree Frog, Giant Tree Frog (Hyla gratiosa).

This large, bumpy-skinned tree frog is found in the Southwestern United States as far West as Louisiana. This frog burrows into sandy mounds during cold weather, and varies in color from bright green to dull gray. Its call is a deep bark. Males 49-68 mm and females 50-68 mm.

Adapted from: *Handbook of Frogs and Toads of the United States and Canada* by Albert Hazen Wright and Anna Allen Wright. (1995)
These activities were adapted from *A Thousand Friends of Frogs' Educator Activity Guide*. This project is run by the Center for Global Environmental Education at Hamline University in St. Paul, MN. For more information, contact A Thousand Friends of Frogs at http://cgee.hamline.edu or call 1-800-888-2182.

Soak It Up

For the past decade, scientists have been alarmed by a dramatic decline in amphibian populations. Amphibians have a two-phased life cycle—terrestrial and aquatic—and permeable skin, both of which make them highly vulnerable to habitat changes and pollutants, both on land and in water.

Selective permeability is critical to frogs and toads. Living in moist areas, toads are able to draw moisture out of the soil and into their bodies through their skin. Just like into the root hairs of a plant, water moves from the soil into the body of a toad. Frogs can live underwater during the winter because they are able to draw oxygen from the water through their permeable skin.

The following activities introduce the concept of selective permeability, and allow students to think creatively about frogs of the future.

Exercise 1: Plump it up.

Peel a hardboiled egg or a raw potato. Measure its circumference and then place it in a jar of water for 24 hours. After observing the egg or potato, describe what is happening. Again, measure the circumference. Explain any changes in size.

Exercise 2: Selective permeability.

Pour orange juice with pulp through a funnel. Describe what happens. Then, pour the orange juice through a sieve or strainer. Now what happens? How does this demonstrate selective permeability?

Exercise 3: What's impermeable?

Pour a spoonful of water on a paper towel and a spoonful on plastic wrap. Which one of these items is impermeable? Choose some other materials and experiment with them; ideas include napkins, sponges, glass, paper, cardboard, cheesecloth, aluminum foil, etc. Rank these materials from least to most permeable. Does everybody agree? For primary grades, it may be a good idea to provide rankings (such as 1 = permeable, 2 = somewhat permeable and 3 = very permeable), and give a demonstration.

Exercise 4: Future frogs of the world.

Imagine that you have the power to control how creatures develop in the future. Design a frog that will be better adapted to conditions in the environment 100 years from now, when the world may be warmer and drier and more polluted. What feature will be important to frogs? Draw your modern frog and describe it.

Exercise 5: Discussion questions

1. How is a frog or toad like an egg or potato?
2. Which materials are most permeable?
3. How are absorption and permeability different?
4. Why is permeability important to frogs and toads? How does it put them at risk?

Take a Good Look

These activities give students a hands-on chance to explore what they already know and to develop and articulate questions. They will also learn about how to contact appropriate experts when answers aren't easily obtained.

Frogs occupy a variety of habitats, and searching in different areas will turn up different species of frogs. Swamps, marshes, streams, and sloughs are good areas because frogs can be seen leaping into the water as people approach. Search your schoolyard or an area park for wet grassy areas; Wildlife Management Areas are good public sites, but they are not always easily accessible.

EXERCISES

Exercise 1: Going frogging.
Be sure to obtain permission from landowners if crossing private property, and be careful with the frogs themselves. At no time should egg masses be disturbed or handled, and frogs should only be held with wet hands that are free of insecticides or sunscreens. Using nets will help students take a closer look at frogs. For human safety, have plenty of adult supervisors when observing near water. Walk slowly, and wade only in shallow water. Be aware of any allergies students may have, such as ragweed or bees, and be prepared to handle any reactions. Also, know hunting seasons in your area and do not go into areas where people may be hunting.

Put on waders or boots and take your students to your nearest pond, swamp, or stream. Look for frogs, tadpoles, and eggs in shallow water in the spring. In the autumn, some frogs can be seen migrating from shallow-water areas to deeper lakes or ponds. When you encounter a frog, be sure to encourage students to take good notes about what they see. Ask for the frog's color, gender (if known), size (from tip of nose to base of spine), type or species, and the number of frogs of each type ob-

served. Do your frogs appear healthy, or abnormal in any way?

Take detailed notes about weather conditions, and describe in as much detail as possible the area in which you observed the frogs. The frog survey form on page 90 may be helpful. Use your notes to make conclusions about the frogs in your area. For example, are there certain frogs that are only seen in water? On average, what is the biggest frog species you saw? What is the most common?

Exercise 2:
Generating questions.
Take a piece of chart paper and write the words Know/Assume at the top. Ask groups of students to list things that they know, or think are true, about frogs and their habitat. Post the chart paper and compare the lists.

With the entire class, generate questions about frogs on a second sheet. Some questions may arise from the Know/Assume lists.

Return to small groups and help students decide which questions can be answered with available reference materials. For example, "What are the differences between frogs and toads?" can be answered by looking

in one of several books on amphibians. However, "What would be the major impact to the ecosystem if frogs were to disappear?" is an evaluative question, and the answer might not be available in written materials. Students should choose questions of interest and commit to finding the answers. Make a list of the questions to be submitted to the experts.

Exercise 3: Ask the experts.
Brainstorm ideas for identifying appropriate experts. With teacher guidance, students may decide on area resources such as university researchers, or representatives from your state Department of Natural Resources or Department of Fish and Game. Encourage students to take the time to organize their questions clearly, and call, write, or e-mail their selected experts. Students may want to ask the same question of more than one person, and compare the answers they receive. The Center for Global Environmental Education at Hamline University runs "A Thousand Friends of Frogs" project; they have a web page and may be helpful in answering some of your questions (contact http://cgee.hamline.edu/frogs or 1-800-888-2182).

Centimeters
0 1 2 3 4 5 6 7 8 9 10 11 12 13 14 15 16 17 18 19 20 21 22 23

FROG SURVEY DATA SHEET

Data Collector Information

Name of organization (if appropriate):_____

Name of youth leader:_____Phone number:_____

Name of observer:_____Phone number: _____

Street address: _____

City/State/Zip code: _____

Time and Location Information

Date and time of observation:_____Weather conditions: _____

Name of the wetland, lake, stream (if appropriate): _____

County:_____Nearest town and direction:_____

Location and type of habitat. (Include township and range if known. Use nearby roads or the name of

the property owner to pinpoint the location.) _____

_____

_____

Frog Observation Information
(If you photograph a frog, use a ruler or a coin to give a size perspective.)

Frog Species*	Size†	Description§
1		
2		
3		
4		
5		

* If unclear, write "unclear."
† Measure from the tip of the snout to the base of the spine; this may help determine the age of the frog.
§ Do you see red on the underside of the thigh or abdomen (this may be "redleg," an infection which can indicate stress)?

Write Away

The Frog Prince, frog games, frog tales, Kermit the Frog. . . these friendly amphibians have always held a special place in the lives and literature of American culture. Help students get started by writing a cinquain, limerick or a How to be. . . poem.

Cinquain

A cinquain poem follows a specific formula. It has five lines, each appealing to the emotions and the senses.

First line: one word, giving the title
Second line: two words, describing the title
Third line: three words expressing an action
Fourth line: four words expressing a feeling
Fifth line: one word, a synonym the title

For each line, ask students to generate possible phrases and to choose the ones they like best.

Cinquain

wetland
mucky gucky
up and down
scared of monsters grabbing
squishy

Joe Heili, age 7

Limerick

Limericks, whimsical and humorous, also follow a set form; the first, second, and fifth lines rhyme; the third and fourth rhyme, too, and are shorter. Choose the name of the person, place, or thing your limerick is going to be about. The trick is to find a number of words that rhyme for lines one, two, and five. Experiment with word order and find synonyms to make the meter work out.

• Create your first line. You may follow the pattern

There once was a _____ named _____ or
There once was a _____ from _____.

• Lines three and four are short lines that rhyme which tell something about your topic.

• For the final line, you may want to repeat the pattern used for the first line.

Limerick

There was an old raccoon named Grog
Whose diet consisted of frog.
He lived near a pond
With the forest beyond
And grew fat on Mink Frog in the bog.

Jessica Cady, age 12

How to be...

Have students choose a topic. Give them time to cluster around their topic, writing down any word associations that come to mind. Ask them to pretend they have the power to teach someone how to become the topic they have chosen. Have them list what one would need to know, what learning would be needed, or how one would act to become this thing. Students could begin each line with learn, or know or be.

How to be...

How to be water.
Learn to flow, slowly and swiftly
Learn to splash and laugh going over rocks
Learn to gather drops of rain from the clouds
Learn to love the fish who live in you.

Herps Bibliography

(Note: A * at the end of a listing indicates that the book is a good source of reptile and/or amphibian pictures.)

GENERAL REFERENCE BOOKS

The Encyclopedia of Reptiles and Amphibians by Tim Halliday and Kraig Adler (Facts on File, 1986)*
A Guide to Amphibians and Reptiles by Thomas F. Tyning (Stokes Nature Guide)(Little, Brown, 1990)

FIELD GUIDES

Familiar Reptiles and Amphibians of North America by John Behler (National Audubon Society Pocket Guide)(Knopf, 1995)
A Field Guide to Reptiles and Amphibians: Eastern and Central North America by Roger Conant and Joseph Collins (a Peterson Guide)(Houghton Mifflin, 1991)*
A Field Guide to Western Reptiles and Amphibians by Robert C. Stebbins (a Peterson Guide)(Houghton Mifflin, 1985)*
National Audubon Society Field Guide to North American Reptiles & Amphibians by John L. Behler and F. Wayne King (Knopf, 1979)*
Peterson First Guide to Reptiles and Amphibians by Roger Conant et al. (Houghton Mifflin, 1992), Advanced*
Reptiles and Amphibians by Herbert S. Zim and Hobart M. Smith (a Golden Guide) (Golden, 1987), Intermediate and Advanced
Reptiles and Amphibians of the World by Massimo Capula (Simon & Schuster, 1989)*
Reptiles of North America by Hobart M. Smith and Edmund D. Brodie, Jr. (Western, 1982)*

CHILDREN'S BOOKS

Alligators by James F. Gerholdt (a Remarkable Reptile book)(Abdo & Daughters, 1994) Primary and Intermediate*
Alligators by Frank Staub (Lerner, 1995), Primary*
Alligators & Crocodiles by Erik D. Stoops and Debbie Lynne Stone (Sterling, 1996), Intermediate*

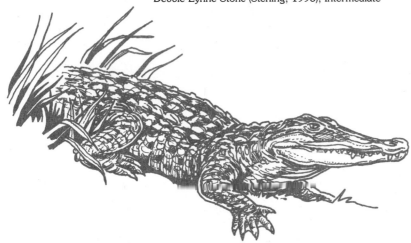

Alligators and Crocodiles (1988), *Snakes* (1991), and *Turtles* (1992) by John Bonnett Wexo (Zoobooks series)(Wildlife Education, Ltd.), Intermediate*
Amazing Snakes by Alexandra Parsons (Eyewitness Juniors)(Knopf, 1990), Intermediate*
Creepy Crawly Things: Reptiles and Amphibians (National Geographic Society, 1974), Primary*
Crocodile and Alligator and Lizard by Vincent Serventy (Animals in the Wild series) (Raintree, 1985, 1986), Primary*
The Fascinating World of Snakes by Maria Angels Julivert (Barrons, 1993), Primary and Intermediate
A First Look at Frogs, Toads and Salamanders by Millicent E. Selsam and Joyce Hunt (Walker, 1976), Primary
Frog by Stephen Savage (an Observing Nature book)(Thomson Learning, 1995), Primary
The Frog: Natural Acrobat by Paul Starosta (Animal Close-Ups)(Charlesbridge, 1996), Primary*
A Frog's Body by Joanna Cole (Morrow, 1980), Intermediate and Advanced*
From Tadpole to Frog by Wendy Pfeffer (a Let's-Read-and-Find-Out Science book)(Harper Trophy, 1994), Primary
A Gathering of Garter Snakes by Bianca Lavies (Dutton, 1993), Intermediate and Advanced
I Wonder Why Snakes Shed Their Skin and Other Questions About Reptiles by Amanda O'Neill (Kingfisher, 1996), Intermediate
The Komodo Dragon by Susan Schafer (Dillon, 1992), Advanced*
Lizards by James E. Gerholdt (a Remarkable Reptiles book)(Abdo & Daughters, 1994) Primary and Intermediate*
Look Out for Turtles! by Melvin Berger (Let's-Read-and-Find-Out-Science Book)(HarperCollins, 1992), Intermediate
Mysteries and Marvels of the Reptile World by Ian Spellerberg and Marit McKerchar (Usborne, 1985), Advanced
Never Kiss an Alligator! by Colleen Stanley Bare (Puffin, 1989), Primary*
A New True Book: Reptiles by Lois Ballard (Childrens, 1982), Primary
A New True Book: Snakes by Ray Broekel (Childrens, 1982), Primary
Outside and Inside Snakes by Sandra Markle (Macmillan Young Readers, 1995), Primary*
Reptile by Colin McCarthy (Eyewitness Book)(Knopf, 1991), Intermediate*
Reptiles by Frank Brennan (Aladdin, 1992), Primary
Reptiles and Amphibians by Louis Sabin (Troll, 1985), Intermediate and Advanced
Sea Turtles by Gail Gibbons (Holiday House, 1995), Intermediate
Snakes by James E. Gerholdt (a Remarkable Reptiles book)(Abdo & Daughters, 1994) Primary and Intermediate*
Snakes by Sylvia A. Johnson (Lerner, 1986), Intermediate and Advanced*
Snakes Are Hunters by Patricia Lauber (Crowell, 1988), Primary
A Snake's Body by Joanna Cole (Morrow, 1981), Intermediate and Advanced*
Snakes: Their Place in the Sun by Robert M. McClung (Henry Holt, 1993), Intermediate
Sssnakes! by Lucille Recht Penner (a Step into Reading book)(Random House, 1994), Primary

Tree Frogs by Sylvia A. Johnson (Lerner, 1986), Intermediate and Advanced*
Turtles by James E. Gerholdt (a Remarkable Reptiles book)(Abdo & Daughters, 1994) Primary and Intermediate*
What Is a Reptile? by Susan Kuchalla (Troll, 1982), Primary
What on Earth is a Chuckwalla? by Edward R. Ricciuti (Blackbirch Press, 1994), Intermediate
What on Earth is a Skink? by Edward R. Ricciuti (Blackbirch Press, 1994), Intermediate
What on Earth is a Tuatara? by Jenny Tesar (Blackbirch Press, 1994), Intermediate
The World of Reptiles by Darlyne Murawski (Ranger Rick ® Science Spectacular Series)(Newbridge, 1996), Intermediate

VIDEOS, FILMSTRIPS, AND SLIDES

Amphibians and Reptiles (Primary)—Musical videos (AIMS Media, 9710 DeSoto Ave., Chatsworth, CA 91311-4409)
Amphibians and Reptiles (Primary)—Filmstrip in the "Animals and How They Grow" series, and *Reptiles and Amphibians* (Advanced), filmstrip in the "Structure of Animals, Part II" series; filmstrips must be purchased in series. *Reptiles* and *Tadpoles & Frogs* (Primary-Intermediate), and *Voyage of the Loggerhead* (Advanced)—Videos with teacher's guides. *Reptiles & Amphibians* (Advanced)—Video or videodisc (National Geographic Society, Educational Services, P.O. Box 98019, Washington, DC 20090-8019)
Atlas of Reptiles and Amphibians, Frogs and Toads, Introduction to the Amphibians, Introduction to the Reptiles, and *Representative Reptiles*—Slide sets (Educational Images Ltd., Box 3456 W, Elmira, NY 14905)
The Chameleon (Intermediate) and *Frogs and Toads—Watch Them Sing!* (Primary)—Videos or films (International Film Bureau, 332 S. Michigan Ave., Chicago, IL 60604)
Crocodiles (Primary), *Giant Turtles* (Primary), *Reptiles* (Intermediate and Advanced) and *Snakes* (Intermediate and Advanced)—Videos (Coronet/MTI Film & Video, 4350 Equity Dr., P.O. Box 2649, Columbus, OH 43216)
It's a Frog's Life (Advanced)—Video detailing the life cycle and adaptability of frogs. This video is long, but contains excellent footage of many species and habits of unfamiliar frogs. Other videos and slide sets also available (Carolina Biological Supply, 2700 York Rd., Burlington, NC 27215)
Videos on reptiles and amphibians—Catalog available from Karol Media, 350 N. Pennsylvania Ave., P.O. Box 7600, Wilkes-Barre, PA 18773-7600

COLORING BOOKS, GAMES, POSTERS, FACT SHEETS, AND CASSETTES

Animal Rummy Cards: Snakes feature snakes, their habits, and habitats in a familiar game. Posters of reptiles and amphibians also available (Carolina Biological Supply Co., 2700 York Rd., Burlington, NC 27215)
Reptiles and Amphibians by Sarah Anne Hughes, Robert Stebbins and Roger Conant, is a Peterson Field

Guide Coloring Book (Houghton Mifflin, 1985)
Sea Turtles of the World Poster, and fact sheet on sea turtles (Advanced) (Center for Marine Conservation, 1725 DeSales St., NW, Washington, DC 20036)
Talking Toads and Frogs Poster—Large full-color poster and cassette of the calls of 25 Missouri frogs and toads (Missouri Dept. of Conservation, P.O. Box 180, Jefferson City, MO 65102-0180)

SOFTWARE

The Animal Kingdom: Amphibians and Reptiles (Advanced)—This CD-ROM, one disk in "The Vertebrates" series, provides a general introduction, narration, tests, facts and printable photos of each species, and an index by species (Educational Images, P.O. Box 3456, Elmira, NY 14905).
The World of Reptiles (Intermediate and Advanced)—CD-ROM provides information about reptiles in general and detailed facts about the life cycles, habitats, and more of individual species. The program features color photos, videos, and narration, and includes quizzes (CLEARVUE/eav, 6465 N. Avondale Ave., Chicago, IL 60631).

OTHER ACTIVITY SOURCES

Amphibians and How They Grow and *Reptiles and How They Grow* (Primary)—"Wonders of Learning" kits containing 30 student booklets, a read-along cassette, and a teacher's guide with activity sheets. Also available on CD-ROM combined with other animal categories (National Geographic Society, Educational Services, P.O. Box 98019, Washington, DC 20090-8019)
Hands-on Nature: Information and Activities for Exploring the Environment with Children—Includes several amphibian activities, created by the Vermont Institute of Natural Science. (To order, write Whitman Distribution Center, 10 Waterman St., 4th Floor, Lebanon, NH 03766).
OBIS (Outdoor Biology Instructional Strategies)—Outdoor activities relating to reptiles and amphibians. "Cool It" introduces temperature variation, and "Leapin' Lizards" looks at lizards out-of-doors; both are part of a module on deserts (Delta Education, Inc., P.O. Box 3000, Nashua, NH 03061).

WHERE TO GET MORE INFORMATION

• college and university departments of biology, zoology, or wildlife
• county or state extension offices
• nature centers
• regional, state, and local herpetology societies
• zoos and natural history museums

Internet Address Disclaimer
The Internet information provided here was correct, to the best of our knowledge, at the time of publication. It is important to remember, however, the dynamic nature of the Internet.
Resources that are free and publicly available one day may require a fee or restrict access the next, and the location of items may change as menus and homepages are reorganized.

Glossary

amphibian—a cold-blooded vertebrate that usually lacks scaly skin, lays jelly-coated eggs in water, and produces mucus and/or toxins from special glands in its skin. Most amphibians go through metamorphosis. Frogs and salamanders are examples of amphibians.

cold-blooded—same as ectothermic.

ectothermic—not being able to internally maintain a constant body temperature. Ectothermic animals' temperatures change with that of their surroundings. Amphibians and reptiles, along with fish and all invertebrates, are ectothermic.

endothermic—being able to maintain a constant body temperature independent of the outside temperature. Mammals and birds are endothermic.

herps—the collective name given to reptiles and amphibians.

Jacobson's organ—a sensory organ, usually in a herp's mouth, that helps a herp smell its environment.

metamorphosis—a process that changes the young of certain animals into their adult forms. Many amphibians go through metamorphosis.

reptile—a cold-blooded dry-skinned vertebrate that usually has scaly skin and typically lays shelled eggs on land. Reptiles do not go through metamorphosis. Lizards, snakes, and turtles are examples of reptiles.

warm-blooded—same as endothermic.

Natural Resources

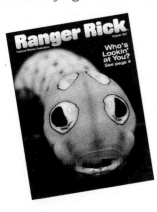